San Francisco

Front cover: the Transamerica Pyramid next to Victorian architecture

Below: Pier 39

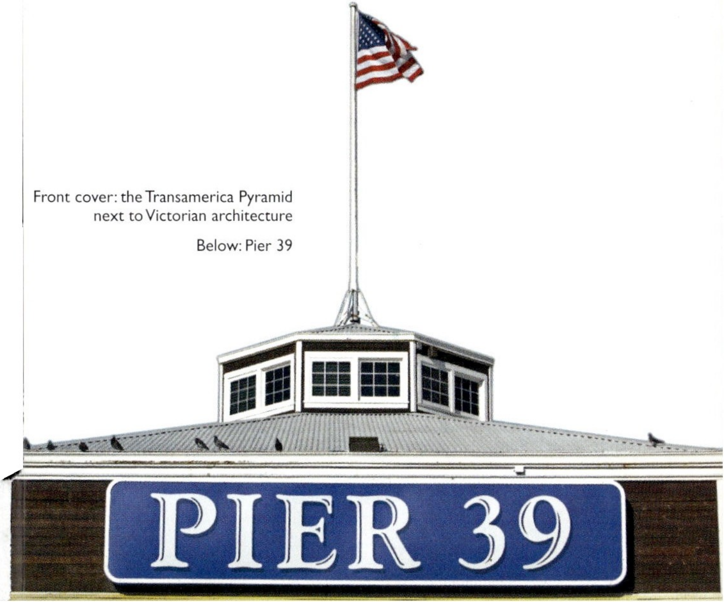

TOP 10 ATTRACTIONS

Chinatown • for colorful facades, sacred temples, herb shops, and dim sum *(page 29)*

Coit Tower • provides various views of the city – both inside and out *(page

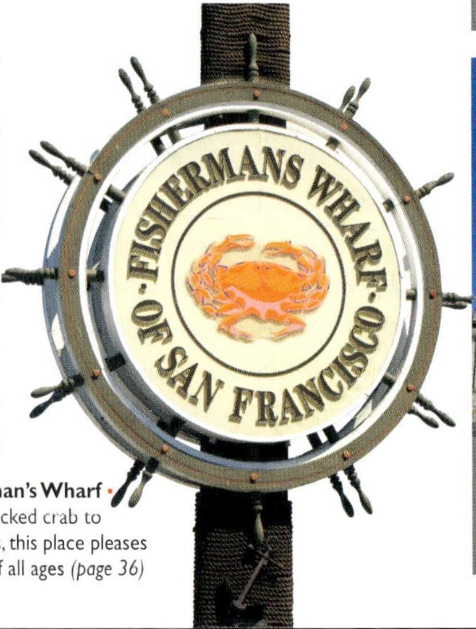

Fisherman's Wharf • From cracked crab to carousels, this place pleases people of all ages *(page 36)*

The Ferry Building • is one the city's architectural gem and a gathering place of all things gastronomic, includi farmers' market *(page 35)*

den Gate Bridge • The ultimate symbol of San Francisco, iconic bridge is an Art Deco masterpiece *(page 45)*

MoMA and the Yerba Buena Gardens • offer cultural and other diversions *(pages 53–4)*

atraz Island • The former son is a brooding presence, of grim fascination and n unparalleled views across bay *(page 40)*

Alamo Square • with its row of 'painted ladies' is one of several classic vantage points in the city *(page 62)*

le Cars • offer stellar views hey traverse the city's endary hills *(page 50)*

Golden Gate Park • has this Conservatory of Flowers, and a celebrated art museum among its attractions *(pages 63–4)*

A PERFECT DAY

9.00am Breakfast

There are two potential ways to start the day: espresso and pastries at classic Caffe Trieste (601 Vallejo Street) or heartier fare at La Boulange (543 Columbus Avenue) in North Beach.

10.00am Steep hills, stupendous views

Stroll across Washington Square then climb Telegraph Hill to Coit Tower. Be sure to view the 1930s murals inside before ascending the elevator for one of the city's most magnificent views. After, walk down the Filbert Street steps with exquisite views of the Bay, to Montgomery Street (or as far as Sansome Street if you feel ambitious) and back.

11.30am To Chinatown

Meander down Grant Avenue past one-of-a-kind boutiques in North Beach to Chinatown's quirky shops. Then feast on savory Chinese dumplings at Gold Mountain (644 Broadway), a cavernous dim sum emporium.

2.00pm Cable car

Hop on a cable car two blocks west at Mason Street and ride past Nob Hill and Union Square. Jump off downtown at the Powell and Market Street turnaround, usually busy with street performers.

2.30pm Coffee and art

Walk three blocks to SFMoMA (closed Wed) and take the elevator to the Rooftop Coffee Bar and sculpture garden for a cappuccino. Then head downstairs to wander through the galleries of renowned modern art.

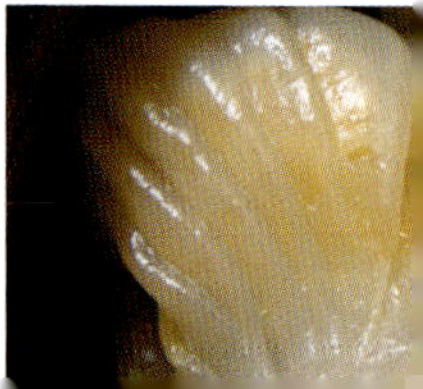

IN SAN FRANCISCO

4.30pm YB Gardens

Cross Third Street in front of the museum to the delightful Yerba Buena Gardens. Roam the gardens and be sure to visit the serenely beautiful Martin Luther King Jr. memorial waterfall. If you need refreshments, relax on the outdoor terrace of Samavor Tea Lounge (730 Howard Street) above.

5.30pm Mega mall

If you have unfulfilled shopping needs, the Westfield San Francisco Centre, with its 270 shops, has it all.

6.00pm Saloon drinks

Step into another era for a pre-dinner cocktail at the friendly Gold Dust Lounge that has been serving libations in Union Square since the end of Prohibition.

7.30pm F-line to Zuni

Board a restored vintage streetcar and zip up Market Street to Zuni Café *(see page 107)* for dinner at this beloved San Francisco culinary institution that serves market-fresh Mediterranean-inspired cuisine. Be sure to book reservations early!

10.00pm Hit the bars

After dinner at Zuni, you are well situated for a night on the town. Grab a taxi and head south to the bohemian Mission bars, SoMa nightclubs, or the lively Castro scene, or take a taxi or bus west to trendy NoPa and the eclectic bars that line Haight Street.

28

30

10

CONTENTS

Features

15

101

88

INTRODUCTION

Earthquakes aside, there's just no shaking off San Francisco. One of America's favorite cities, San Francisco clings to your soul, as irresistibly as a yen for the good things in life, or a song that won't vacate your head. The ballad may be syrupy, but so many millions of people have left their hearts in San Francisco that you can't fight it: the City by the Bay incites love at first sight – a love that lasts.

Hills and Thrills

The first astonishment is the setting. So many thrillers have been filmed in San Francisco that the hills look as familiar as home; and yet it turns out that the cameramen didn't need trick lenses; the hills are just as giddily steep as in the movies. Officially, 43 hills stand up to be counted, most famously Nob, Russian, Telegraph, and Twin Peaks. From these vantage points the views are endlessly varied and stimulating – the magnificent Pacific, the choppy bay and its mysterious islands, and other hills dotted with mansions, eccentric Victorian houses, or skyscrapers with character. And if somewhere in the world there is a more noble bridge than the Golden Gate, its glory isn't crowned with wisps of fog.

The sound of a foghorn is as much a San Francisco particular as the clang of a cable-car bell. First heard in the 1870s, that bell still incites the squeals of tourists hanging on as the cable car rounds a bend. More subtly, you can hear the actual cable speeding under the street at a relentless 9½mph (15km/h), perpetually protesting like a distant alarm clock. A more piercing aural trademark is the tweet of the tin whistle of a hotel doorman commanding a taxi in the sunshine, or

San Francisco at dusk

pleading for one in the drizzle. In ethnic neighborhoods the sounds are as exotic as the hiss of a North Beach espresso machine or the slurping of soba noodles in Japantown.

Even in summer – more so in summer, when much of California is broiling – the San Francisco weather is invigorating. Thanks to a temperate marine climate, as it's called, the mercury rarely tops 70°F (21°C) at any time of year. Thus, except for the more arduous hills, which are best tackled by cable car, taxi or bus, San Francisco is definitely a city for walkers. How else could you appreciate the architectural adventure of the high skyscrapers in the Financial District, the abundance of Italian cafés in North Beach, or the pungent aromas of Chinatown?

An aging hippie enjoying the sunshine at a San Francisco café

Diversity and Tolerance

San Francisco has always been a melting pot, especially since international fortune-hunters flooded in to exploit the gold rush of the mid-19th century. At the moment, the largest single ethnic group in the city is Chinese, though every culture in the world seems to be represented, as evidenced by the mushrooming roster of ethnic restaurants, from Afghan to Vietnamese.

Home-grown Americans from all parts of the country keep moving in, attracted by the scenery, the eternal springtime, and a truly cosmopolitan atmosphere in a city of just over three-quarters of a million people. Another intangible inducement is a very civilized tolerance. San Francisco respects its minorities of all stripes, including starving artists, splinter-party politicians, and militant homosexuals.

Food heaven

Renowned for the quality and quantity of its restaurants, at 5,300 and counting, San Francisco has more restaurants per capita than any other major city in the United States.

From the social summit of Nob Hill to the ethnic patchwork of the Richmond District, the neighborhoods of San Francisco have their own distinct personalities. If you were lost in the retro Haight-Ashbury District, you'd certainly get the impression it wasn't tidy Noe Valley. Meanwhile, Russian Hill and the Mission District are as different as New York's Upper East Side is from the Lower East Side.

All this is going on in a relatively compact corner of the West Coast, the tip of the peninsula. The city itself covers about 49 sq miles (120 sq km) – one-tenth of the area of Los Angeles. To put it into a more metropolitan context, the region is considered to include Oakland, San Jose, and the rest of the nine-county Bay Area, totaling 6 million people. Even so, the resident population is outnumbered by the annual tourist influx by a ratio of more than two to one.

Camouflaged by Fog

San Francisco Bay, a naval, commercial, and recreational haven of 496 sq miles (1,285 sq km), went undiscovered until rather late in the colonization of America. For a couple of centuries, Spanish, Portuguese, and English sailors must have sailed on past the Golden Gate, where the Pacific meets the bay, but it seems to have been fogbound every time. Finally, in 1769, the

Spanish pioneer Gaspar de Portolá exclaimed over a harbor big enough to shelter all the navies of Europe. It was a sort of back-door discovery, for his party stumbled on the bay from land, not sea. Seven years later Spanish colonists arrived, set up a fort, and built a mission to convert the local Native Americans. Mission Dolores, which is still here, was dedicated to St Francis of Assisi, or, as they say in Spanish, San Francisco.

By 1846, when the town, then ruled by Mexico, was claimed by the United States, there was nothing much to brag about – a trading post with fewer than 1,000 inhabitants. Two years later, a revolution was sparked by a four-letter word: gold. The bonanza on the American River, 140 miles (225km) away, catapulted San Francisco to the status of an international dream. And there was no looking back.

Shaky Grounds

The threat of earthquakes is all too real for the people of San Francisco, as everyone was tragically reminded in 1989, when

Waiting for the Next Big One

San Francisco sits right on top of the San Andreas Fault, a major fracture in the earth's crust that runs northwest from the Gulf of California for 600 miles (965km), passing beneath the city and separating Point Reyes from the mainland. The BART subway tunnel between San Francisco and Oakland was bored right through the fault.

The Baja California peninsula and the coast west of the fault are moving north relative to the rest of North America, at an average of half an inch (1cm) per year. There has been no movement along the San Francisco section of the fault since the disastrous earthquake of 1906, but citizens live with the constant threat of another major earthquake – the dreaded Big One. New buildings are built to stringent structural standards, and much money is spent retrofitting older structures.

the city trembled at a shrug of the San Andreas Fault. Seismological phenomena are a fact of life in California, where some people wait for the Big One with the fatalism of a fisherman in a typhoon.

The earthquake of October 1989 was far less terrible than the catastrophe of 1906 that became the great dividing line in San Francisco's history. On that occasion thousands of men, women, and children lost their lives, fires burned for three days, and the city was all but wiped out.

Still standing: the city's Victorian heritage

Many hundreds of Victorian landmarks were preserved or restored, but what replaced the rubble was an elegant 20th-century city, worthy of its position as unofficial capital of the American West. Culture is thriving in San Francisco, with its opera, symphony orchestra, ballet, theaters, museums, and universities, and spills over into the areas of refined shopping and eating.

Like its setting and its history, San Francisco is romantic, but with so much to see and do, the pace can become hectic. For relief, cross the bay to the heavenly sanctuary of the redwoods, the sunny valleys of vineyards, or waterside villages that seem more Mediterranean than Californian. On the return journey, soak up the mood of the harbor, its islands, sailboats, and ferries, and the San Francisco skyline, a thrilling clash of high-rise majesty, low-slung homes, and sprinkles of parkland. If there were nothing here but 43 bare hills, it would still be a marvel.

A BRIEF HISTORY

Until the American Revolution, the San Francisco Bay Area, isolated by ocean and mountains, languished in prehistoric obscurity. While 18th-century Bostonians were going to Harvard, humming the catchy music of the young Mozart, the inhabitants of this region were fishing and trapping. They were Native Americans of the Ohlone and Miwok tribes, so far removed from modern influences that they had never seen a horse or a wheel.

Not until 1776 did the first colonists – the Spanish – arrive at what is now San Francisco, where they built a presidio, or military garrison, and a religious mission to convert and educate the Indians. Settlement began seven years after the first Europeans had discovered the mighty bay. Ships from many European nations, sailing up and down the Pacific coast, had been missing the Golden Gate for centuries, probably because of the fog. The best-known explorer to come close was Sir Francis Drake, who is said to have landed farther north in 1579 at what is now Drake's Bay.

In the early years the Spanish colony showed no particular promise. The presidio, overlooking the Golden Gate, was never called on to repel invaders; the commander was reprimanded during the late 1700s when he twice entertained the captain of a British Royal Navy ship, thus disclosing his unpreparedness.

Meanwhile, inland, the mission went about its evangelical work, but many Indians died as European diseases rampaged through their population.

Mexicans and Gringos

California came under Mexican control in 1822, when Mexico won its independence from Spain. A few years later the new regime secularized the network of California missions, including Mission Dolores. The Church's extensive lands were reassigned to settlers, some of whom amassed huge cattle ranches. With the Franciscan friars out of a job, the native Indians tragically lost direction, caught halfway between the old and the new civilizations.

While the presidio was impressing nobody and the mission was declining, a live-wire English sea captain, William Richardson, founded a more promising settlement – starting with his own tent – near the sheltered Yerba Buena Cove. The cove disappeared long ago as landfills pushed back the sea from hills considered too steep to make settlements on. In fact, the site of Richardson's tent is now high and dry in the middle of Chinatown.

The American era began on July 9, 1846, in the early stages of the Mexican War, when the *USS Portsmouth* sailed through the Golden Gate. The sloop's captain, John Montgomery, led a party ashore and raised the Stars and Stripes flag over the plaza, now called Portsmouth Square after the ship. The ship's cannon then saluted the change of proprietorship. Captain Montgomery himself is immortalized in the name of Montgomery Street in the Financial District. The peace treaty of Guadalupe Hidalgo was signed on February 2, 1848, nine days after gold was discovered in California.

Inside Mission Dolores

Bonanza!

The starter's gun for California's lusty gold rush was fired far from civilization, halfway between Sacramento and Lake Tahoe. At a lumber mill in the Sierra foothills, a carpenter named James Marshall glimpsed the sparkle of the first nugget on January 24, 1848. His boss, the pioneering tycoon John Augustus Sutter, helped with chemical tests confirming that this was the genuine 23-carat article. Breaking their conspiratorial silence, Sutter soon spread the word.

At first, the reaction in San Francisco was skeptical. Then an ironmonger and huckster, Sam Brannan, appeared in the center of town with a bottle of nuggets, shouting, 'Gold! Gold from the American River!' By no coincidence, his sales of shovels and pickaxes picked up instantly. Brannan went on to become the city's first millionaire. Gold, then silver, made San Francisco the capital of the American West.

The city was virtually abandoned overnight as every ambitious, able-bodied citizen rushed to the goldfields. They were followed by the so-called 'Forty-Niners,' eager prospectors lured from as far away as Australia, China, and Europe. Thousands more boarded ships in New York for the daunting four- to six-month voyage around the tip of South America to San Francisco. On arrival, many a sailor jumped ship at San Francisco and joined the rush for the 'Mother of all Lodes.'

The population of the shantytown of San Francisco doubled overnight, then doubled again. In a few months

A dubious trade

Lured by saloons, gambling houses, opium dens and brothels, unsuspecting sailors drawn to the Barbary Coast were at risk of being slipped 'Mickey Finns' – opium-laced whiskey – and shanghaied (kidnapped) and forced on lengthy sea voyages. Skippers paid crimps up to $75 a head to supply them with able-bodied men to crew the vessels.

San Francisco around 1850

an overgrown hamlet of 2,000 people became a rugged city of 20,000. Before the gold rush fizzled, hundreds of thousands of hopefuls had passed through San Francisco, enriching every entrepreneur from bootmaker to brothel-keeper. It was a wild time, with shortages of everything – housing, food, and law and order – the perfect climate for fast profits.

Real-estate speculators, gamblers, money-lenders, and merchants prospered much more handsomely than the miners. None more so than a Bavarian immigrant named Levi Strauss, who sold the miners overalls that could stand up to the hardships of the Sierra. They were fashioned first from bolts of brown canvas sailcloth, but after demand began to outstrip supply, Strauss switched to a sturdy cotton fabric with a similar weave to that of a material produced in Nîmes, France. *Serge de Nîmes*, as it was called, was soon shortened to 'denim.' With the addition of rivets to give extra strength to the pockets, Levi's jeans were born.

Golden State

California was coining precious metals so fast that the US Congress granted it statehood in 1850. After the gold ran out, a bonanza of silver, known as the Comstock Lode, followed. Providing the mining equipment and infrastructure for the Virginia City adventure, San Francisco became the fourth-busiest port in the nation, a real town with hotels, theaters, and hundreds of saloons. There were however side-effects: overcrowding, crime, immorality, and exploitation. It was also a time of disastrous fires, many the work of arsonists. With its haphazardly built shacks, fragile oil lamps, and a tendency for windiness, the town was extremely vulnerable to fire. Crime was a real cause for concern, and the citizens rallied with vigilante groups. If this resulted in the odd lynching, San Franciscans chalked it up to a worthy trend toward an orderly society.

San Francisco drew closer to the rest of the United States in the 1860s with the opening of a direct telegraph line to New York and, at the end of the decade, of the rail link that joined the Atlantic to the Pacific. Four Sacramento merchants, whose names are still affixed to California institutions,

City Planners

The layout of San Francisco's streets – grandly logical, on paper – goes back to the early days of Yerba Buena. In 1839 a Swiss settler, Jean-Jacques Vioget, drew up a plan for a town, basing it on the Spanish model of a large town square from which streets radiated in a grid.

Under American rule in 1847, an Irish surveyor, Jasper O'Farrell, was given the project of extending the plan. He 'invented' Market Street and the much bigger blocks to the south. Both planners were more interested in theory than in practice, which is why the city's long, straight streets go over the tops of hills instead of circling around them. O'Farrell's additional gift to modern motorists is the struggle to find a way to cross Market Street joined forces to build the Central Pacific railroad. They were Charles Crocker, Collis P. Huntington, Mark Hopkins, and Leland Stanford. Their scheme, generously subsidized by the US government, finally came to fruition at Promontory, Utah, in May 1869, when the 'golden spike' symbolically spliced eastern and western lines. The 'Big Four' entrepreneurs profited a great deal from their monopoly, and the railroad opened the way for unemployed Easterners to descend on the golden West, thus depressing wages, prices, and the economy in general.

The Central Pacific Railroad

That the railroad could be built at all was thanks to Chinese workers who had begun arriving in California after the 1849 rush. While they had met considerable hostility from Americans and Europeans working the Mother Lode, the Central Pacific found that the Chinese were the best laborers for laying track through hair-raising mountain terrain. Eventually, more than eight out of ten workers on the line were Chinese. Once the project was finished, unemployed Chinese flooded the California job market, prompting more discrimination. Most of the Chinese stopped trying to compete and retreated to their own enclave, San Francisco's Chinatown.

Golden Years

In the 1870s and 1880s, San Francisco took on the air of a real city, the key to the West, with a population in the hundreds of thousands and amenities to match. Work on Golden Gate Park, destined to become one of the nation's biggest and best municipal parks, was begun in 1870. City transport took a great leap forward in 1873 when the first cable cars made Nob Hill effortlessly attainable. Next, trolleys brought the more distant areas within reach, and land prices boomed.

The financial prowess of the city was confirmed when a stately United States Mint was built at Fifth and Mission streets. The granite fortress processed a fortune in gold and silver from area mines, producing coins that filled the banks (and pockets) of the West. The Pacific Coast Stock Exchange was founded in 1875, the same year that the luxury Palace Hotel, built at a cost of 5 million dollars, first opened its doors. Among other elements of modern design it was meant to be earthquake-proof; it survived the quake but then succumbed to the ensuing fire.

The Great Earthquake

As San Francisco slept, early in the morning of April 18, 1906, the clocks stopped at 5.12. If there had been a Richter Scale in those days, it would have registered about 8.3. The Great San Francisco Earthquake fissured streets, toppled chimneys, and crumbled thousands of houses, but the worst was yet to come. As gas mains broke, fires erupted – but the water mains also ruptured. The San Francisco Fire Department, whose chief was one of the first victims, could do little to control the flames. The great fire roared out of control for three days and wiped out 4 sq miles (10 sq km) of the heart of the city. Crowded aboard ferries heading for Oakland and Marin County, the city's

Up in smoke

'Within an hour after the earthquake shock the smoke of San Francisco's burning was a lurid tower visible over a hundred miles away. And for three days and nights the lurid tower swayed in the sky, reddening the sun, darkening the day, and filling the land with smoke… San Francisco is gone. Nothing remains of it but memories…'

Jack London, May 5, 1906.

refugees looked back at an apocalyptic skyline under a pall of black smoke.

The final death toll was at least 3,000. With a quarter of a million San Franciscans homeless, most of them camped out in Golden Gate Park, there was huge pressure to rebuild. Reconstruction pushed ahead, and within three years the disaster area had been reclaimed. A clean-up of a different sort brought the downfall of the corrupt regime of Mayor Eugene Schmitz, although His Honor himself managed to avoid jail.

To demonstrate to the world that recovery was complete, the Panama-Pacific International Exposition was held in San Francisco in 1915. It celebrated the opening of the Panama Canal, but more than that the rebirth of a great city. When the tourists had all gone home, the Barbary Coast nightlife scene was finally tamed under the state legislature's red-light abatement law. With a population of half a million, San Francisco had come a long way from the days of the Wild West.

The Call Building burns after the 1906 earthquake

Depression and War

During the Great Depression of the 1930s, ambitious public-works projects were designed to provide employment for workers with many skills. The interior of the Coit Tower on Telegraph Hill, dedicated in 1933, was adorned with frescoes by local artists; Franklin Roosevelt's New Deal paid their salaries. The 1930s also put brawnier workers on the payroll, constructing two great bridges: the San Francisco-Oakland Bay Bridge, and the much shorter, but more glamorous, Golden Gate Bridge. The two opened only six months apart. In a mood of growing optimism, yet another San Francisco World's Fair, the Golden Gate International Exposition, was held.

The biggest job-provider of all, World War II, came soon enough. The threat to San Francisco was perceived to be real, and the city staged its first blackout alert only one day after the Japanese attack on Pearl Harbor, in December 1941. San Francisco played a big part in the war effort as a military and industrial base. As hundreds of Liberty ships rolled from Bay Area assembly lines, 1.6 million American fighting men were funneled through Fort Mason on ships heading for the combat zones. After Japan surrendered in 1945, the UN Charter was signed in San Francisco.

Coit Tower mural

Beatniks and Hippies

San Francisco had always had more than its share of nonconformists; the new breeds evolving after the war provoked the world's fascination if not admiration. First came the Beat Generation, later known disparagingly as 'beatniks.' Congregating in North Beach *(see page 48)*, they dressed like revolutionaries, drank coffee while discussing philosophy, read and wrote poetry (some memorable), and supported the avant-garde jazz scene.

A symbol of rebellion

In the 1960s the action shifted to the low-rent Haight-Ashbury district *(see page 62)*, where a new species of rebel, less productive intellectually, came to be called 'hippies.' Ideological powerhouses in San Francisco and Berkeley inspired student radicals all over the United States with their demonstrations for improved civil rights and against American involvement in the Vietnam War. After the US pulled out of Vietnam, the city's image as a hotbed of radicalism refocused on a wave of gay-rights agitation. In 1978, the first official in the US to proclaim his homosexuality, City Supervisor Harvey Milk, was assassinated, along with Mayor George Moscone. A lenient sentence for the assassin – a disaffected politician – spurred violent protests.

Shaken Again

Earth tremors are a familiar phenomenon in California, but the quake that struck on October 17, 1989, registering 7.1 on the Richter Scale, was the most severe tremor since 1906, causing billions of dollars' worth of damage and claiming 67 lives. Earthquake-proof modern buildings survived, but many older houses suffered, and a large section of the double-decker Bay Bridge collapsed. The elevated Embarcadero Freeway was damaged as well, and the eyesore was subsequently dismantled. In a fitting bit of irony, the earthquake can be credited for liberating a long-ignored corner of the city in the decade that followed, paving the way for waterfront development, additional public transportation routes, and a brand-new ballpark.

Boom and Bust

The first two years of the 21st century were heady times for the technology industries in the city and especially in nearby Silicon Valley. Companies both large and small made millions from ideas that dominated the Internet and became the basis of the 'new economy.' The dot-com bubble finally burst on October 9, 2002, resulting in one of the biggest stock market crashes of all time.

Gone were the flashy cars, unlimited expense accounts, and overpriced apartments. An atmosphere of recovery and fresh ideas began to replace the 'get-rich-quick' mentality among the young high-tech generation. An above-average number of underemployed twentysomethings contributed to a passionate mayoral election between the Green Party candidate, Matt Gonzales, and Democratic Party front-runner Gavin Newsom, both in their mid-thirties. Newsom won and immediately began shaking up City Hall. On February 12, 2004, 15 same-sex couples were married, and dozens of marriage licenses to same-sex couples were issued, sparking controversy and national debate. Under Newsom's tenure, dealing with the homelessness problem has been a priority, and San Francisco has become a shining example of 'green' practices.

A San Francisco couple

Historical Landmarks

1769 Spanish soldier José Ortega discovers San Francisco Bay while on a scouting mission for Gaspar de Portolá, governor of Spanish California.
1776 On June 29, the first Mass is conducted in San Francisco on the site of Mission Dolores.
1846 During the war with Mexico, Captain John B. Montgomery arrives at the site of today's Portsmouth Square and claims the town of Yerba Buena for the United States.
1847 Yerba Buena renamed San Francisco.
1848 James Marshall discovers gold in the Sierra Nevada foothills, prompting the great gold rush of 1849.
1873 Andrew Hallidie's cable car takes its inaugural run down Clay Street on August 2.
1906 Two tremors hit San Francisco in the early morning followed by three days of fire. The city is virtually destroyed.
1915 The city hosts the Panama-Pacific International Exposition.
1936–7 The San Francisco-Oakland Bay Bridge opens in 1936, followed in 1937 by the Golden Gate Bridge.
1945 The United Nations Charter is signed by representatives from 50 countries in the War Memorial Opera House on June 26.
1967 Golden Gate Park is the site for the 'Human Be-In,' and the Haight-Ashbury neighborhood becomes a draw for hippies.
1978 Former City Supervisor Dan White assassinates Mayor George Moscone and gay City Supervisor Harvey Milk.
1989 A 7.1 earthquake hits the city.
2000 A new Muni route down the Embarcadero to Fisherman's Wharf opens after two years of construction. The San Francisco Giants baseball team plays its first season at Pacific Bell Park.
2004 Mayor Gavin Newsom licenses the marriage of thousands of gay and lesbian couples, sparking a national debate.
2007 The city celebrates the 40th anniversary of the 'Summer of Love.'
2010 The San Francisco Giants win the World Series, a first for the city in baseball's ultimate contest.

WHERE TO GO

With its well-oiled if oft-maligned public transportation system, all of San Francisco is easy to reach. And once you're in the neighborhood you want, it's a great walking town. Walking tours proliferate, targeted at a broad spectrum of interests, from the historical and architectural to the literary or culinary and ethnic.

However, before you start off, it's wise to get your bearings with a half-day coach tour. Considering all the hills and the fact that the city is surrounded on three sides by water, its geographical subtleties are not instantly apparent; many a first-time visitor, admiring the steel span of the Bay Bridge, thinks that it's the Golden Gate. Another worthwhile orientation exercise is a one-hour harbor tour, featuring views of the San Francisco skyline. For the price of an all-day Muni pass you can see a great deal of the city using buses, street cars, and cable cars. Driving around in traffic-heavy San Francisco is not recommended, and locating a parking place is only for the most determined of individuals.

So many hotels, shops, and attractions are centered in Union Square that we begin our survey of San Francisco's sights here. You might want to do the same, as the Visitor Information Center of the San Francisco Convention & Visitors Bureau is right at hand *(see page 128)*, at 900 Market Street, near the Powell Street cable-car terminus in Hallidie Plaza at Market and Powell streets. They can supply you with brochures, maps, and answers to your questions.

The Golden Gate Bridge

Urban utopia

'San Francisco is 49 square miles surrounded by reality.' Paul Kantner, singer, guitarist and co-founder of the psychedelic San Francisco rock band Jefferson Airplane.

DOWNTOWN

Union Square

London has Regent Street, and New York Fifth Avenue. San
1 Francisco does its fashionable shopping around **Union Square**. Big names include Tiffany's, Saks Fifth Avenue, Neiman-Marcus, Macy's, Cartier, Barneys, and Gucci. In recent years a new crop of stores, including Niketown and Levi's, have joined such hot spots as H&M, Goorin Brothers, and Forever 21 to take the staid edge off the square.

Surrounded by slow-moving traffic, including a cable-car line, the square sits right on top of the nation's first underground parking garage. It was reopened in 2002 after a multi-million-dollar facelift which got rid of most of the grass. The statue of Victory atop the Corinthian column in the center celebrates Admiral George Dewey's 1898 Manila Bay victory during the Spanish-American War.

Victory in Union Square

A landmark on the west side of the square, the **Westin St Francis Hotel**, first opened for business in 1904. Rebuilt, overhauled, expanded, and refurbished over the years (the lobby alone cost $2 million in 1991), the hotel has welcomed many royals, heads of government, and celebrities. Dozens of hotels, from five-star palaces to modest rooms with shared facilities, are found within a five-minute walk of Union Square. The area is also populated with many of San Francisco's homeless, who make their appeal to the consciences of the city's well-heeled passers-by.

On the east side of the square, **Maiden Lane** runs into Stockton Street. The prim name is an affectation. Maiden Lane was once known as Morton Street, under which alias it was a hotbed of Barbary Coast vice, most notably prostitution. The post-earthquake fire of 1906 extinguished the red lights, and nowadays it's a pleasant and well-appointed pedestrian street of designer shops.

Maiden Lane's shops

The building at 140 Maiden Lane that houses the Xanadu Gallery is the only San Francisco work by the architect Frank Lloyd Wright. The ramp is reminiscent of Wright's revolutionary Guggenheim Museum in New York.

Chinatown

Immerse yourself totally in the experience and lose yourself in the 24-square-block confines of San Francisco's **Chinatown**. Here the second-biggest Chinese community outside Asia (New York's is first) crowds into the exotic emporia, temples, tea houses, and restaurants. By way of infrastructure there are Chinese banks, schools, law offices, travel agencies, video shops, bookstores, laundries, and factories recalling the sweatshops of earlier times. 2

Since gold-rush days, most of the Chinese in San Francisco, and the United States in general, have had their roots in Guangdong (Kwangtung) province, whose capital is Guangzhou (Canton). Thus the Cantonese dialect and cuisine are often encountered here. But newer immigrants from other Chinese provinces, and from Indochina, Hong Kong, and Taiwan, have added their own distinctive flavor to the melting pot.

In order to enter Chinatown through the front door, approach it from the Union Square area or the Financial District. The **Chinatown Gate**, at Grant Avenue and Bush Street, has the classic design of a Chinese village gate, but it dates from 1970. Bulging with souvenir shops and restaurants, always bustling Grant Avenue is the prime tourist promenade of Chinatown. But be sure to veer off to find a more authentic experience on Broadway and Stockton Street and the tiny alleyways in between.

Bustling Chinatown

Two blocks ahead, across the California Street cable-car tracks, **Old St Mary's Church** was San Francisco's Roman Catholic cathedral during most of the second half of the 19th century. Now it is a parish church. Under the clock is an inscription, 'Son Observe the Time and Fly from Evil.' That's 'son,' not 'sun' – it was aimed at prospective patrons of the brothels that used to operate across the street.

Chinatown Gate

Portsmouth Square, where slow-motion t'ai chi exercises are performed and old men play chess, happens to be very important historically. This was the main plaza of the original Mexican colony that became San Francisco. The square sits atop a parking garage and features a children's playground, benches, and a perfect view of the Transamerica Pyramid in the Financial District.

The **Bank of Canton** at 743 Washington Street preserves the delightful **Old Chinese Telephone Exchange** in the original, spectacularly Chinese setting of red pillars and soaring tile roofs. This was the headquarters of the Chinatown telephone exchange, where operators could deal with subscribers in English as well as in Chinese dialects. After World War II the arrival of dial telephones put these talented linguists out of work.

The backstreets of San Francisco's Chinatown meet almost all specifications for those in search of the mysteries of the Far East. **Ross Alley**, up Washington Street from Grant Avenue has garment factories, jewelry shops, sellers of miniature Buddhist shrines, and a one-chair barber shop. Here, too, is the Golden Gate Fortune Cookie Company, from where those typically American-Chinese sweets originate. Watch the deft hands of the operators folding moist cookies around slips of paper enigmatically foretelling the fate of future customers at Chinese restaurants around the world. You can purchase bags of fresh almonds or fortune cookies from the ladies in the factory.

Although Grant Avenue constantly teems with tourists, **Stockton Street** is busier still; it's where the Chinese community shop for food and essentials. Soak up the sights, sounds, and smells of Chinese supermarkets, open-air vegetable markets, fish markets, herbalists, delicatessens, pastry shops, and tea rooms. On the roof of the modern Chinatown branch of the US Post Office at Stockton and Clay streets is a Chinese temple – the **Kong Chow Temple** – with a historic altar and a view of the bay from its balcony. At 843 Stockton Street, the headquarters of the **Chinese Six Companies** (officially the Chinese Consolidated Benevolent Association) is a garishly decorated building dating from the early 20th century. The organization was central to the fight against anti-Chinese discrimination.

Financial District workers

Financial District

Heading northeast into the Financial District, stop in the **Crocker Galleria**, an airy, glass-domed shopping mall on three floors. It was inspired by Milan's Galleria Vittorio Emanuele, built more than a century earlier. Across Sutter Street from the mall, don't miss the **Hallidie Building**, named after the man who put the cable car on track. Dating from 1917, it might have been the first 'glass curtain wall' building anywhere; the glass-and-metal facade hangs from the top instead of helping to support the structure. Apart from the boldness of the engineering, there are wonderful frills, such as the disguised external fire escapes. The ground floor of the Hallidie Building is now shared by a bank and a post office. Office workers take their lunch breaks on **Belden Place**, off Bush Street between Pine and Kearny streets. Here, half a dozen delicious restaurants offer outdoor dining.

The Transamerica Pyramid

Reaching a height of 850ft (260m) and with 48 floors, the **Transamerica Pyramid** is the highest building in San Francisco. When it was built in 1972, it caused much controversy. Many residents felt that it spoiled their beautiful city, while purists regarded the plans by William Pereira Associates as typical of crazy Californians. But the work went ahead, and it is now impossible to imagine the city without the pyramid's distinctive spire dominating the skyline. 3

Place names in San Francisco tend to be straightforward, but just as North Beach is not a beach, **Jackson Square** is not a square. The name refers to a block of buildings bounded by Jackson, Montgomery, Gold, and Sansome streets, just north of the Transamerica Pyramid. The city's pioneers crudely reclaimed this area from the bay with ballast from arriving ships, and in many cases the ships themselves, abandoned by crewmen who joined the gold rush. This was destined to become one of the most infamous areas of the Barbary Coast. A relatively small collection of low-rise, thick-walled brick offices, banks, shops, and factories miraculously withstood the quake and subsequent fires in 1906. In the middle of the 20th century, when the district's historic and architectural importance was discovered, restoration of the landmarks began. Today, Jackson Square has become the elegant place to have a law office, ad agency, art gallery, or antiques shop.

Shopping at the Embarcadero center with the Ferry Building

BESIDE THE BAY

The Embarcadero

San Francisco's big, beautiful waterfront got a major facelift when the 1989 earthquake doomed the elevated Embarcadero Freeway, an eyesore that cost nearly half as much to dismantle as it did to build. With the demise of the 'abominable autobahn,' as the San Francisco *Chronicle* called it at the outset, unobstructed views of the Ferry Building and harbor were revealed, and local developers and planners took a long, hard look around. They eventually decided to install a length of new Muni tracks, along with inviting plazas on which you can linger while you admire the imported palm trees that decorate the boulevard. Called **The Embarcadero** (Spanish for 'wharf'), this piece of the bay stretches from the baseball stadium at King Street all the way to Fisherman's Wharf.

You'll get a dramatic view of the **San Francisco-Oakland** 4
Bay Bridge rumbling almost overhead near Harrison Street. The bridge, anchored in the middle on Yerba Buena Island, is 8 miles (13km) long. Like the more celebrated Golden Gate Bridge, it was built during the Depression days of the 1930s. Unlike the Golden Gate, the Bay Bridge wears a necklace of lights to add to the romance of San Francisco's nights.

Just northwest of the bridge's take-off for Oakland is the
Ferry Building, where you may board a Golden Gate com- 5
muter ferry to Sausalito, Tiburon, Larkspur and locations in the East Bay. The landmark building and its impressive bell tower date from the turn of the 20th century; the latter was modeled after the Giralda, the 12th-century bell tower of Seville Cathedral in Spain, and its clock is the largest dialed, wind-up, mechanical clock in the world. Today the building is a destination for 'foodies' both local and far-flung, who come to dine at one of the restaurants, shop for gourmet food and top-of-the-line kitchen accessories, and browse the impressive, pricey farmers' market (Tue and Thur 10am–2pm, Sat 8am–2pm; free; www.ferrybuildingmarketplace.com).

Walkers, joggers, bicyclists, and skateboarders make the most of The Embarcadero's wide sidewalks. The maritime industries that made this a significant port, have either disappeared or moved to the railhead at Oakland across the bay. What's left are the ferries, luxury liners welcoming passengers bound for Alaska and other destinations in the Pacific, harbor cruise ships, sightseeing boats, and deep-sea fishing and whale watching charters.

Sea lions basking at Pier 39

Fisherman's Wharf

California's most visited attraction is Disneyland, which can be an expensive family outing; in second place is San Fran-
6 cisco's **Fisherman's Wharf**, which is free, sort of. The area of amusements, souvenir shops, bongo drummers, mimes, and generally unstoppable street life runs along Jefferson Street from around Pier 43 to beyond Pier 47.

7 **Pier 39**, a tourist complex constructed of recycled lumber from old wharves, is the major draw, with millions of visitors a year. They come to shop, snack, or dine, watch street performers, ride a double-deck carousel, admire the view of the bay, take a tour, rent a yacht, or discover what all that barking is about. No, that's not a pack of eager hounds on K-Dock, but up to 600 sea lions preening themselves and arguing over the best spot to sunbathe.

At the heart of it all is a concentration of fish restaurants. Local gourmets may look down on them, citing that their prices are high for preparations that are quite pedestrian. Nevertheless, they're handy places for fresh local and imported seafood with a view. The 'fast food' offered by outdoor stalls here – shrimp and crab cocktails, and clam chowder in an edible bowl – is popular, but if crab isn't in season (November through May), those crustaceans you're eating have been frozen. The truth is, the fishing fleet that you can see here contributes only a small percentage of the catch needed to feed San Francisco.

At Pier 45, a boat of a different sort is worth a look. ***USS Pampanito*** (May–Oct daily 9am–8pm, Wed 9am–6pm, Oct–May Sun–Thur 9am–6pm, Fri–Sat 9am–8pm; charge; www.maritime.org), a World War II submarine credited with the sinking of six Japanese ships, is open to visitors (admission is charged). Even though the sub is not submerged, some landlubbers feel a touch of claustrophobia in the narrow passages and dimly lit operations center.

Also moored here at Pier 45 is the Liberty Ship *SS Jeremiah O'Brien*, a veteran of the D-Day invasion of France and a memorial to the World War II personnel of the US Merchant Marine. More than 2,700 such ships were produced between 1941 and 1945. Pier 45 is also the home of the

Persistent Pinnipeds

The bewhiskered sea lions have been barking at Pier 39 since 1990, evidently attracted by a herring bonanza and a totally safe, comfortable haven. Although the big fellows put a potentially profitable yacht-parking zone out of action, nobody could convince them to leave, and federal law forbids harassing them. Pier 39 discovered that the smelly squatters were good for business; a sculpture was commissioned as a tribute to the blubbery marine mammals, and for tourists who want to know more about their swimming, feeding, and breeding habits, there are explanatory tours.

Musée Mécanique, housing more than 300 historic mechanical relics from penny arcades ranging from orchestrions, coin-operated pianos, antique slot machines, and animations, down to small dioramas. It's a refreshing, nostalgic alternative to the contemporary digital video arcade.

Inland from Fisherman's Wharf, the **Cannery** occupies a vast red-brick building from the early 20th century. It was an important fruit-packing plant, cleverly converted into an attractive browsing, eating, and entertainment area.

Ghirardelli Square is a bigger shopping and eating zone, housed in a former chocolate factory. A stylish alternative to the knick-knack-and-T-shirt boutiques of Jefferson Street, the enterprises here sell toys, jewelry, fashionable clothes, and even museum-worthy folk art from several continents, as well as chocolate – although the well-regarded local brand is now manufactured in a high-tech plant across the bay.

Victorian Park, overlooking the Aquatic Park Marina and the bay, is a pleasant place to break from the heavy footwork of sightseeing and shopping. Flocks of tourists spend more time than they had planned in this park, queuing up for the cable car. This is where the Powell-Hyde line is pushed onto the turntable before heading back toward Union Square.

Parts of the stunning Art Deco **Aquatic Park Bathhouse** 8 are open while undergoing renovations in stages, and the Maritime Park's Visitor Center nearby at 499 Jefferson Street (at Hyde) offers high-tech ex-

Local specialty

Those in need of a pick-me-up before braving the Powell-Hyde cable-car line should head to the nearby Buena Vista Café, for one of the legendary libations produced and perfected there. The combination of espresso, Irish whiskey, cream, and sugar, known as 'Irish Coffee,' is a true San Francisco treat.

hibitry that tells the story of San Francisco's colorful and diverse maritime heritage (daily 9.30am–5pm; free; www.maritime.org). Exhibits here tell the stories of voyage, discovery, and cultural diversity. Since 1849, the world has rushed through the Golden Gate, and each wave of population or industry has left its own fascinating imprint.

The *Balclutha* at Hyde Street Pier

Real historic ships, rocking gently against the pier, 9 are near at hand at **Hyde Street Pier**, part of the Maritime National Historic Park (daily May–Oct 9.30am–5.30pm, Oct–May 9.30am–5pm; charge; www.maritime.org). More than a century old, the sidewheel ferry ***Eureka*** was the world's largest passenger-and-car ferry in its day. Vintage cars are parked aboard, as they were when the ferries constituted a link in US Highway 101. Other old ships that you can board include the ***C.A. Thayer***, a three-masted lumber-carrying schooner, as well as the ***Balclutha***, a square-rigger launched in Scotland in 1886.

West of the piers is nearby **Fort Mason** (www.fortmason.org), which was headquarters of the San Francisco Port of Embarkation during World War II. Over 1.5 million troops and 20 million tons of cargo passed through here on their way to combat zones. After the war, operations shifted to

Alcatraz, sometimes referred to as 'the rock'

Oakland, and now the fort is part of the Golden Gate National Recreational Area.

At sea level, a complex of nine buildings is now devoted to entertainment, recreation, and education, as well as other cultural initiatives and Greens, an upscale vegetarian restaurant. Art spaces that currently operate in the Fort Mason Center include the Museo ItaloAmericano (Tue–Sun noon–4pm; free; www.museoitaloamericano.org) and the SF Museum of Modern Artists Gallery (Tue–Sat 11.30am–5.30pm; free).

Alcatraz

All harbor excursions offer a close look at the brooding former prison isle called **Alcatraz**, but the only way to step ashore and tour the abandoned cell blocks is via the Hornblower Fleet from Pier 33 (daily; charge; tel: 888-814-2305; www.alcatrazcruises.com). In summer and at weekends the tours are soon sold out; you have to book early, sometimes weeks ahead. For a truly remarkable experience, check out one of the spooky yet beautiful night tours. Also ask about tours for children.

The vital difference between Alcatraz, sometimes referred to as 'the rock,' and its French equivalent, Devil's Island, is that Alcatraz looks out on a seductive city, not a hostile jungle; with the wind in the right direction, the prisoners could even hear the sounds of civilization just beyond their reach. Alcatraz (from the Spanish *Isla de los Alcatraces*, or Pelican Island) served as America's most forbidding federal penitentiary from 1934 to 1963. It's said that Attorney General Robert Kennedy closed down the dilapidated prison when he discovered that it would have been cheaper (and certainly more comfortable) to keep the inmates at the Waldorf Astoria Hotel. Now the island is operated by the US National Park Service. A self-guided trail has been laid out, covering the principal areas of interest, or you can join in a more specialized walking tour led by a park ranger. Inside the cell blocks, you can rent an audio tour (available in English, French, German, Italian, Japanese, and Spanish), on which tour directions are interspersed with a documentary based on the

Escape from Alcatraz

Officially, nobody ever escaped from Alcatraz. In all, 39 prisoners attempted it: 27 were caught, seven were killed, and five have never been found but are assumed drowned.

In 1962, at the very end of the prison's grim history, John Paul Scott made it to the San Francisco shore by greasing his body to help withstand the cold. A party of students found him clinging to the rocks at Fort Point, just below the Golden Gate Bridge, completely exhausted. Not knowing he was an escaped prisoner, they helpfully called the police to rescue the poor fellow in his hour of need.

pertinent testimony of retired wardens and ex-prisoners. You'll see the cells of Al Capone and 'the Birdman,' Robert Stroud; roam the central corridor, ironically known as Broadway; have a chance to step inside a solitary-confinement cell; and check a typical menu in the dining hall. Alcatraz food is said to have been the best in the federal prison system – designed to give the inmates one less reason to riot.

By one count, 39 prisoners tried and failed to escape from the island. Two made it to the mainland, only to be picked up almost immediately, and five are listed as missing, officially presumed drowned – but did they? Here the imagination takes over.

Palace of Fine Arts

Marina District

The earthquake of 1989 put the Marina on the world's television screens: because the district is built on land reclaimed from the bay, dozens of houses succumbed to the 7.1 shock. The land was created from dredged sand after the 1906 quake to provide a site for the Panama-Pacific International Exposition of 1915.

Other than the earthquake problem, the Marina is a desirable place to live or visit, with its charming pastel-painted houses and varied upmarket shopping on Chestnut Street. **Marina Green** is a fashionable bayside park for sunbathing, jogging, skating, biking, and kite-flying.

An eye-catching monument from the 1915 World's Fair, the splendid pink
11 **Palace of Fine Arts** designed by Berkeley architect Bernard Maybeck, restored and reinforced, survived the tremor of 1989. This was a lucky development, for both its dreamy contribution to local pseudo-classical architecture and its utility. The palace now houses the **Exploratorium** (Tue–Sun 10am–5pm; charge; www.exploratorium.edu), a museum of science, art and human perception. Even an inquisitive octopus would not get his fill of 'hands-on' exhibits at this endlessly instructive and entertaining center. Children become animated and intent, and parents and grandparents insist on their turn. Founded by Dr Frank Oppenheimer (brother of the atomic Robert), the institution amounts to a big workshop.

Wave Organ

Out on a jetty that juts into the bay near the yacht club in the Marina is a fascinating wave-activated acoustic sculpture known as the Wave Organ, built of granite and marble from a demolished cemetery. Listen at high tide to the subtle rumblings of a watery symphony.

The Presidio

Hundreds of thousands of invigorating cypress, eucalyptus, and pine trees shade the 1,480 acres (600 hectares) of the
Presidio of San Francisco, the prettiest ex-military establishment you're ever likely to see. 12
Founded as a Spanish fort in 1776, then active on the American side in several wars, it was belatedly converted to civilian life during the 1990s as part of the Golden Gate National Recreation Area. The beauty of the landscape dates from the late 19th century, when the trees were planted on what had been forbidding, rocky heights.

Running along the tree-lined Presidio

Feel free to explore the Presidio, by bus or car or on foot, for its tastefully designed and impeccably maintained headquarters buildings, officers' quarters, and even model enlisted men's barracks.

The San Francisco National Cemetery is the final resting place for some 450 'Buffalo Soldiers' – African American servicemen. Not far away is an army pet cemetery, rich in anecdotal dog and cat gravestones.

Once forlorn and decaying, the Presidio has undergone much development over the past decade. In 2005 George Lucas, of Star Wars fame, moved the headquarters of Lucasfilm into the Letterman Digital Arts Center housed in buildings that artfully blend with the centuries-old Presidio architecture. Since then, cafés, restaurants, a yoga studio, a high end spa, and a sporting goods store have opened within the vast confines. The Presidio is also home to Baker Beach on the western edge, as well as a popular children's playground, golf course, bowling alley, and hiking and bike trails.

Hiding under the southern end of the Golden Gate Bridge, mid-19th-century **Fort Point** (Thur–Mon 10am–5pm; free; www.nps.gov/fopo) is an ominous-looking relic with a heart-stopping view of the strait. The National Park Service now runs tours through what was once the US Army's only brick fortress defending the West Coast against naval attack. The threat was considered real at the time of the Civil War, when it was suspected that the Confederate Navy might show up. As in so many military designs, this coastal artillery installation became out of date technologically as soon as it was built. Engineering enthusiasts will appreciate the almost-close-enough-to-touch view of the underside of the great bridge. Candlelight tours are offered monthly. For information and reservations on these and other tours, tel: 415-556-1693.

Golden Gate Bridge

Perhaps **Golden Gate Bridge** is thrilling because the pylons, as tall as 65-story buildings, taper upward like the spires of an Art Deco cathedral. It's not just the grace of its arches, though; you have to see the fog devouring its towers while the sun flashes on the water below, where sailboards zigzag in and out of the wake of ferryboats. Whatever the magic, one of America's favorite bridges is a wonder of engineering. In the little park at the southern end a statue honors the designer, Joseph B. Strauss of Chicago, also responsible for the Arlington Memorial Bridge in Washington, DC. 13

Looking down on the Golden Gate

Here you can see and touch a sample cross-section of one of the cables supporting the bridge – composed of 27,572 wires for a diameter of 3ft (0.9m).

Chief Engineer Strauss began promoting the idea of a bridge in 1917. Many opponents of the project feared a bridge would deface the dramatic strait; others simply felt it couldn't be done, as tidal currents sometimes reach 60mph (100km/h). After 'two decades and 200 million words,' as Strauss put it, the people believed him. Construction began in 1933. Eleven construction workers died, but 19 others were saved by the safety net Strauss designed. The bridge opened for traffic in May 1937.

A bridgeworker's job is never done, of course, so a crew of more than 40 is occupied year-round to clean and paint, using some 5,000 gallons (22,730 liters) of paint per year. The color, called 'international orange,' is the most easily visible in fog, and has won prizes for resisting salt, rain, sun, and wind.

Charles de Gaulle walked across the bridge in 1960. So can you, in either direction. It's about a 2-mile (3km) trip – an invigorating, windy outing for the whole family. But leave behind anyone with a fear of heights; it's about 220ft (67m) straight down to the water, and you can feel the bridge swaying.

The Bridge: the Score

When it was built, the Golden Gate Bridge was the world's longest and tallest suspension structure. Here are some statistics:

Total length (including the approaches): 8,981ft (2,737m).

Height of towers: 746ft (227m).

Total weight on San Francisco pier foundation: 363,000 tons (329,000 metric tons).

Total length of wire in cables: 80,000 miles (129,000km).

Traffic per year: approximately 40 million vehicles.

Fare: $6 arriving in San Francisco; leaving town it's free.

THE HILLS

Coit Tower, with statue of Christopher Columbus

The hills of San Francisco provide uplifting views of the city and the bay – just the thing for millionaires in search of a homestead or tourists merely wanting to borrow a panorama. Of the 40 or so hills available, we've chosen a few of the most appealing, with some detours into the valleys.

Telegraph Hill is named after the primitive semaphore set up here in gold-rush days to relay news of ship arrivals to traders down in the Financial District. In 1876 a group of benefactors bought the top of the hill and gave it to the city for a park. Students of architecture and landscaping will be delighted to see how it turned out; the houses and gardens clinging to the hillsides are charmingly original. For a good look, walk the **Filbert Street steps** down to Sansome Street and return via the Greenwich Street steps where you can admire lush, hidden away gardens. 14

Sprouting from Telegraph Hill is the landmark **Coit Tower** (daily 10am–6pm; charge for elevator to top), a reinforced-concrete column of no practical value but considerable grace. Notwithstanding the version often recounted by tourist guides, it was not designed to resemble a fire-hose nozzle. It was merely an artful way of fulfilling the bequest of Lillie 15

Hitchcock Coit, an unconventional 19th-century woman with close ties to the fire brigade, to build a beautiful monument. You have to pay to ride to the top for one of the best vantage points in town, but there is no charge to view the fine WPA murals created under the supervision of Diego Rivera, which depict California life during the Great Depression years in Socialist Realist style, in the lobby.

North Beach

A landlocked valley between Telegraph Hill and Russian Hill,
16 **North Beach** is not a beach at all. Although Chinatown is making inroads, this is the heart of the Italian community, where Columbus Day is a very big deal. North Beach is the place to find real Italian *prosciutto*, *gelato*, and *cappuccino*. It was once also the focus of the city's artistic and intellectual life, where poets, Bohemians hung out and influenced the culture.

Washington Square with Church of Saints Peter and Paul

The center of the neighborhood is **Washington Square**, a small park with Benjamin Franklin in the middle. People from Chinatown arrive in the morning to do tai chi. The changing complexion of the area is also reflected in the **Church of Saints Peter and Paul**, where one of the morning Masses is said in Chinese every Sunday.

City Lights Bookstore in North Beach

North Beach's main street, Columbus Avenue, has several claims to fame. Lawrence Ferlinghetti's **City Lights Bookstore** was the headquarters of what became known as the Beat Generation, and earnest intellectuals still take seats there and browse. Other thinkers and escapists stake out the nearby cafés, rich in Italian aromas and heady atmosphere. One further cultural note: A **plaque** set on the wall of the Condor nightspot at Broadway and Columbus claims that this is the birthplace of both topless (in 1964) and bottomless (1969) entertainment.

Russian Hill

You're unlikely to find any Russians on genteel Russian Hill, or no living ones anyway. In the earliest days of San Francisco this was a burial ground for the crews of Russian trapping and fishing ships. The very top, bounded by Francisco, Hyde, Lombard, and Taylor streets, is best reached by public transportation, due to driving and parking problems. Some of the streets are so steep they simply turn into stairways. As for streets that are fit for cars – with very brave or foolhardy drivers at their wheel – have a look at Filbert

Street, which is between Leavenworth and Hyde streets. The grade here is 31.5 percent, the steepest in the city, according to the Municipal Bureau of Engineering. If you insist on driving along it, be sure your brakes are in top-notch condition and take the crest *very* slowly.

17 Another amazing thoroughfare is the 1000 block of **Lombard Street**, the 'crookedest street in the world,' between Hyde and Leavenworth. To ease the stress, eight switchbacks were installed, cutting the incline to a mere 18 percent. Among

Cable Cars

A genuine National Landmark on the go! If you thought cable cars were just a tourist gimmick, don't mention it to the San Franciscans aboard. It's quite clearly one of the most enjoyable and exciting ways to travel, and one that simply must be experienced.

Whether crammed into the passenger compartment, braving the elements on benches facing outwards, or even standing on the running board and hanging on, you could never have known that 9½ mph (15km/h) would feel so reckless. The crewmen are gregarious, and chat and joke with the passengers, but they are very stern about where you sit or stand; follow their orders.

The cable cars themselves are powerless. To travel, the gripman has to clamp onto the moving cable, which propels the car until he releases the grip and signals to the brakeman to apply the brakes. The grip mechanism and the brakes have to be replaced quite often, and when a cable breaks everything must stop until it can be mended.

Outrageously out of date, the cable-car system has on occasion been threatened with closure for efficiency reasons, but in 1964 the cable cars were added to the National Register of Historic Places. In the 1980s all the lines were shut down for nearly two years for top-to-bottom renovation. The ancient cars are too close to San Francisco's heart to be endangered again for a long time.

architectural highlights, see the **Octagonal House** at 1067 Green Street, which was built before the Civil War. At the time there was a theory that eight-sided houses were better for the health than the usual quadrangular design. The only other house of this kind here is 2645 Gough Street (second Sun and second and fourth Thur every month, noon–3pm; closed Jan and holidays; tel: 415-441-7512 for tour reservations; free).

Cars navigating the twists and turns of Lombard Street

Nob Hill

The 'nob' in **Nob Hill** is short for 'nabob,' an old-fashioned English word from India for a rich and powerful man. The nabobs who settled on this smart California Street hilltop had made their fortune in the gold-rush days, as often as not in the railroad business. All four rail barons – Charles Crocker, Mark Hopkins, Leland Stanford, and Collis P. Huntington – built private palaces here in the 1870s, as the newfangled cable car was then making the hill accessible. Three of them now have their names attached to luxury hotels on Nob Hill, the exception being Charles Crocker, whose family very generously gave their land as the site of Grace Cathedral. 18

Today, five-star hotels and elite apartment blocks have displaced all the old mansions, except one. Behind its brass filigreed fence, the **Pacific Union Club** at 1000 California Street was once the 42-room home of one James Flood, a saloon-keeper who became one of the kings of the Comstock

Silver Lode. Although the interior of the mansion was gutted in the 1906 fire, its brownstone sobriety remains intact. This traditional gentlemen's club, also known as the P-U, is one of the city's most exclusive. Unlike the club, the fashionable hotels of Nob Hill admit women. In fact, just about anyone can slip into the hotel lobbies or have a drink in any of the attractive bars.

Grace Cathedral (Mon–Fri 7am–6pm, Sat 8am–6pm, Sun 7am–7pm; free; www.gracecathedral.org), an Episcopalian tribute to Gothic style, was built in 1964. Although it does resemble Notre-Dame of Paris, this impressive church is built of concrete and steel – not stone – as an anti-earthquake precaution. The gilded bronze doors of the east entrance are replicas of the 15th-century *Gates of Paradise* sculpted by Lorenzo Ghiberti for the Baptistery in Florence. Two intricate and beautiful labyrinths – one inside and one out front – draw visitors, who walk the winding paths for both enjoyment and meditation.

MARKET STREET

Mostly as straight as an arrow, the wide diagonal of Market Street marches from the bay-front at the **Ferry Building** *(see page 35)* right to the edge of Twin Peaks. It starts promisingly among ambitious skyscrapers, then rambles on through the sort of neighborhood you wouldn't want to linger in.

One of San Francisco's most distinguished structures is the **Hobart Building**, located at Market and Montgomery streets. It was designed by Willis Polk, a leading architect in the rebuilding of San Francisco after the 1906 earthquake, and was the city's tallest building when completed in 1914. At Market and New Montgomery is the **Sheraton Palace Hotel**, the city's original luxury hotel. Its awesome, glass-domed Garden Court is a sumptuous setting for breakfast, tea, dinner, or just a peek at how the other half lives. The contemporary **San Francisco Marriott Hotel**, at Market and Fourth, contrasts with its daring postmodern design. Some critics think it looks like a 40-story jukebox.

View to Market Street with the Hobart Building (left)

A shopping mall with a distinctive flavor is the
19 **Westfield San Francisco Centre** (note the British spelling, which is supposed to add to the upmarket feeling). It has raised the tone at Fifth and Market streets with its magnificently restored Deco escalators, still a source of amazement for many visitors. The top five floors all belong to the Nordstrom department store. A stunning, full-scale $460,000 expansion in 2006 added movie theaters, 110 new stores, restaurants, and the largest Bloomingdale's outside of New York City.

South of Market

Not long ago, South of Market Street, or **SoMa**, had been in upheaval, as gentrification razed buildings and raised rents in what had long been a sketchy and underprivileged neighborhood. It quickly became the city's hippest enclave and the center of Internet activity. The biggest of the projects that
has revolutionized the area is **Yerba Buena Gardens**, and 20

the nearby **Moscone Convention Center**, named after the assassinated Mayor George Moscone *(see page 23)*. It is an enormous exhibition complex, mostly underground, and big enough to hold a political convention. The lovely gardens have brought a welcome presence to the area, along with enough amusements to keep visitors busy for an entire day. For youngsters, there's a carousel that originally graced the long demolished Playland at the Beach, an ice-skating rink, bowling alley, and **Zeum**, a hands-on technology and arts center specifically geared to older kids and teenagers. On the northwest corner, you'll no doubt be drawn toward the **Metreon**, an entertainment complex with 15 theaters (including an IMAX) and a few restaurants.

The most prominent building nearby is the stunning **San**
21 **Francisco Museum of Modern Art** (MoMA; Sept–May Fri–Tue 10am–5.45pm, Thur until 8.45pm, June–Aug Fri–

Face to face with modern art at SFMoMA

Tue 11am–5.45pm, Thur until 8.45pm; charge; www.sfmoma.org), whose works include paintings and sculptures by Matisse, Klee, Pollock, and other major artists of the modernist schools; included, too, is an extensive collection of photography. In the daytime, art-lovers come here to inspect the galleries, shop in the gift store, and lunch in the café.

Free admissions

Some of the city's best museums offer visitors free admission days. SFMoMA, the de Young, the Palace of the Legion of Honor and the Asian Art Museum are free on the first Tuesday each month. The Academy of Sciences and the Exploratorium are free on the first Wednesday each month.

The nearby **Museum of Craft and Folk Art** (Wed–Sat 11am–6pm; charge; www.mocfa.org) is situated on Yerba Buena Lane, a charming pedestrian walkway that connects Market and Mission streets. Relocated from its previous home in Fort Mason, the museum showcases innovative exhibits of traditional and contemporary art and craft from all over the world.

Yerba Buena Lane is also the address of the **Contemporary Jewish Museum** (Fri–Tue 11am–5pm, Thur 1–8pm; charge; www.thecjm.org). In a striking architectural mashup of traditional and modern architecture designed by Daniel Libeskind, the Jewish Museum features traveling exhibitions that explore Jewish culture, history, and art.

At 685 Mission Street, the **Museum of the African Diaspora**, aka MoAD (Sun noon–5pm, Wed–Sat 11am–6pm; charge; www.moadsf.org), opened its doors in late 2005. The museum is dedicated to celebrating the universal connection of all people through their association with Africa, the cradle of humankind. Through programs focused on art, history, and culture, MoAD aims to help impact the view of the modern world and the global family.

Tucked inside a rather nondescript building a half-block from the Metreon is the **Cartoon Art Museum** at 655 Mission Street (Tue–Sun 11am–5pm; charge; www.cartoonart.org). Endowed by *Peanuts* creator Charles M. Schulz, the museum is a treasure trove of artwork and books, featuring underground and mainstream cartoonists.

SoMa is also known for its thriving nightlife – ranging from *Sex and the City*-style hotel bars to pumping dance clubs to trendy, acclaimed restaurants. Here you'll find cutting-edge cuisine, all-night gay dance clubs, hip cafés, porn shops, industrial live/work spaces, and furniture stores that cater to the modern aesthetic.

The South Beach District borders SoMa and is home to AT&T park, where 2010 World Series Champions, the San Francisco Giants baseball team play from April to September. What was once a decaying maritime area of lonesome piers and abandoned brick buildings with the wistful charm of Jack London and Jack Kerouac's San Francisco, now sparkles with glass high-rise condominium towers, new restaurants, and money.

Dolores Park in the Mission District

NEIGHBORHOODS

Mission District

Mission Street runs parallel to Market Street until Van Ness Avenue, where it bends into a north–south direction and becomes the main stem of the Mission District. It is an ethnically diverse area, the neighborhood of choice for Mexicans, Central and South Americans, and San

Franciscans seeking somewhat affordable housing.

Located on Dolores Street at 16th Street, **Mission Dolores** (daily 9am–4pm, except for major holidays; donation suggested; www.missiondolores.org), otherwise known as the Mission of San Francisco de Asís, is a great little survivor. This most venerable building in San Francisco still stands, evocative of the atmosphere of 18th-century Spanish colonial life. The adobe church at the mission is a more modest affair than the basilica next door, which is an elaborate Churrigueresque revival monument built to replace the brick Gothic church that was destroyed by the 1906 earthquake.

Mission Dolores

22 The restored ceiling of the elongated, narrow church of Mission Dolores is decorated with brightly colored Indian motifs; the carved altars came from Mexico. A small museum on the premises shows how the California missions were constructed, and there is a collection of photographs of a visit here by the Pope in the 1980s. A walled-in cemetery beside the church also serves as a botanical garden, a restful place with more than 100 varieties of flowers, most of them in bloom. A statue of the founder of the mission system, Father Junípero Serra, was the work of blind sculptor Arthur Putnam.

Hispanic heritage

Precita Eyes Mural Arts (www.precitaeyes.org) is an organization dedicated to preserving San Francisco's many magnificent murals depicting the social, religious, and political artwork of the Mission's Hispanic community. They offer guided tours to ferret out these colorful gems; but the best-known mural block is found on Balmy Alley (between 24th and 25th streets).

The merchants along **24th Street** east of Dolores Street call their thoroughfare the Mission District's 'Boulevard of the Americas,' and a Mexican national holiday is celebrated here on May 5 *(see page 97)* with a colorful parade. There are dozens of brilliantly tinted Mexican-style murals, as well as plenty of exotic grocery stores and restaurants offering Mexican cuisine. West of Dolores Street on 24th Street is the central artery of **Noe Valley**, a neighborhood of Victorian houses, cute boutiques, and lots of moms pushing strollers.

Civic Center

Monumental grandeur is the keynote of the San Francisco Civic Center, built after the 1906 quake with unbounded optimism and funds. The scope and size of this center of municipal government can't be matched anywhere else in the United States.

23 **City Hall** resembles the Capitol building in Washington, but the black-and-gold dome of the San Francisco structure (patterned on St Peter's in Rome) is even higher. Inside the great rotunda, over the clock, is inscribed the name of James Rolph, Jr ('Mayor 1912–1931'). Surely any first-class dictator would envy 'Sunny Jim' Rolph this monument; the ceremonial staircase all but cries out for magnificent evening gowns and tails.

The **Main Public Library** occupies a faux-Beaux-Arts building across from its former genuine Beaux-Arts headquarters, which reopened in 2003 as the **Asian Art Museum** 24 after a dramatic revamp that blends the former Beaux-Art design with stunning modern elements. The collection includes more than 16,000 objects from China, India, Iran, Japan, Korea, the Himalayas, and Southeast Asia. The broad concourse flanked by trees and fountains is the **United Nations Plaza**, named after the world organization founded in San Francisco in 1945. It is the scene of a farmers' market on Wednesday and Sunday.

On Van Ness Avenue, behind City Hall, an ensemble of nicely balanced buildings includes the **Opera House**, **Symphony Hall**, and the **California State Office Building**.

Castro

This is a friendly neighborhood, well stocked with coffee shops, boutiques, and bookshops, but you'll soon notice something is different. Castro Street is the main street of the district most closely associated with San Francisco's gay community – which constitutes a numerically and politically significant proportion of the city's population. The biggest annual parade in San Francisco is the Lesbian/Gay/Bisexual/Transgender Pride Celebration in June, which involves the participation of hundreds of thousands of people of many orientations.

Along Castro Street

When the Muni Metro train stops at Castro Street station, you surface in **Harvey Milk Plaza**, which is named after the first openly gay elected official in the United States. He was martyred in the City Hall assassination of 1978. The wittily named specialized shops of Castro Street are the most unusual monuments, except for the classic 1920s cinema palace,
25 the **Castro Theatre**, in a lavish, ornate pre-Art Deco style. At 1800 Market Street, the **San Francisco Lesbian, Gay, Bisexual and Transgender Community Center** promotes a dynamic range of activities that support the community.

Up the hill from here, **Twin Peaks** are not quite the tallest hills in town, but nearly. The lucky folk whose houses are perched on the hillsides enjoy unparalleled views of the San Francisco skyline and the bay.

Japantown

A modern interpretation of a five-tiered round pagoda towers above Japantown, or Nihonmachi (between Geary, Webster, California and Octavia streets), where the city's sizeable Japanese population comes to stock up on ethnic food, books, and films. The **Peace Pagoda**, a gift from the people of Japan, is surmounted by a graceful nine-ringed spire symbolizing the highest virtue and supporting a golden sphere with a flaming head.

Japanese people have lived in San Francisco since the 1860s, though their numbers have dwindled significantly over the years. The darkest era was World War II, when Japanese-Americans were sent to internment camps. After the war, many returned, however, and during the 1960s the Japan Center transformed the area into a commercial zone with shopping malls, offices, sushi bars, restaurants, and a hotel and spa. Bibliophiles will enjoy browsing in the **Kinokuniya** bookstore, an enormous bookshop specializing in books and magazines about Japan.

Just east of Japantown, at Gough and Geary streets, **St Mary's Cathedral** is the city's most unusual religious structure, replacing a smaller Catholic cathedral destroyed by fire in 1962. Its modern architecture zooms heavenward. American and Italian architects and engineers joined forces in geometric experiments – the cupola is described as a hyperbolic parabola, with a volume of nearly 2,135,000 cubic ft (60,000 cubic m). The ingredients combine in a harmonious whole, with red-brick floors, wood, glass, reinforced concrete, and marble. Covering two city blocks, the cathedral can accommodate 2,400 worshippers, seated on three sides of the altar. The modern organ, built in Padua, Italy, counterpoints the architectural innovations; it has 4,842 pipes.

A monument in Japantown

Pacific Heights

For mansion-watchers, rubbernecking in the Pacific Heights district is more gratifying than in Nob Hill. There's an extraordinary collection of dream houses along Broadway and Vallejo streets built by wealth and well endowed with good taste. Architectural features, down to the window shutters and doorknobs, are as original as the flower beds and the shrubbery. Many of the fine Edwardian and Victorian homes have remained in private hands, while others function as schools, museums, or consulates.

One of the advantages of living in Pacific Heights is the ready availability of wide-open spaces for walking the dog, playing tennis, or gazing at the skyline. Covering four blocks with trees, flowers, and grass, **Lafayette Park** is the highest of the area's hilltop parks. Another treat afforded by this charmed summit is a superior view of Alcatraz *(see page 40)* – just behind the **Spreckels Mansion**, built by one of the sugar barons and currently owned by the novelist Danielle Steele. Modesty has never entered the picture here, and the house might be mistaken for a neoclassical bank or opera house.

Another mansion that is full of character is the **Haas-Lilienthal House** (guided tours Sun 11am–4pm, Wed and Sat noon–3pm; charge; www.sfheritage.org/haas-lilienthal-house) at 2007 Franklin Street, dating from 1886. Its design is a conglomeration of geometrical shapes – cubes, triangles, cones, and cylinders. Although it is now occupied by the Foundation for San Francisco's Architectural Heritage, you can rent the ballroom for private special events.

Alta Plaza is another Pacific Heights hilltop park of note, steeply terraced and with fine views. Due south, in the West-
26 ern Addition, keen photographers head for **Alamo Square** for the picture-perfect row of admirably restored and filigreed Victorian houses affectionately known as the 'painted ladies' in the foreground, with the elegant downtown skyline.

Haight-Ashbury

The golden age of Haight-Ashbury is long over, but the reputation and the smell of patchouli incense linger on. You'll notice among the passers-by that there's a high percentage of people on another wavelength, and way too many panhandling teenagers. Fond memories of Flower Power and the Summer of Love are recalled in the esoteric shops.

The 'painted ladies' of Alamo Square

Rebels with flowers in their hair took over the district in the 1960s, pursuing noble goals and, on a more individual level, comprehensive hedonism. The world's infatuation with the counter-culture lifestyle eventually cooled, however, and nowadays nostalgia has taken over. Aging hippies, twentysomething fashionistas and multiply-pierced hipsters mix with goth kids and homeless punk rockers among the funky boutiques, kitschy novelty stores, head shops, psychedelic poster and art galleries, bookstores, and organic grocers along Haight Street. The world's largest independent music store, Amoeba Music, anchors the western end of the street.

Golden Gate Park

One of the largest man-made parks in the world unfolds right from the edge of Haight-Ashbury to the Pacific Ocean. **Golden Gate Park** is by any standard a triumph of landscaping.

Drifting dunes have been transformed into an oasis covered with trees and shrubs of every shade of green, flowers that always seem to be in bloom, and lawns that make you want to run barefoot over them. Recreational activities to suit a wide range of ages and tastes are sprinkled liberally across the park's 1,017 acres (412 hectares), along with several first-class cultural attractions.

27 The **California Academy of Sciences** reopened in the park in 2008 and has been packed ever since. The greenest museum in the world combines a natural history museum, planetarium, aquarium, and world-class research facility under a sod-covered 'living' roof.

28 Built in 1878–9, the **Conservatory of Flowers**, a copy of the famous Palm House in London's Kew Gardens, is the oldest building in the park and houses rare and exotic plants and tropical flowers.

29 One of San Francisco's primary art museums, the **M.H. de Young Memorial Museum** (Tue–Sun 9.30am–5.15pm, Fri 9.30am–8.45pm; charge; http://deyoung.famsf.org) was damaged in the 1989 earthquake and reopened in 2005 in a state-of-the-art new facility that has captured the imagination of all who visit by cleverly integrating art, architecture, and the

Out of the Dunes

They laughed in 1870 when civil engineer William H. Hall said San Francisco's barren 'Outside Lands' could be reclaimed and turned into a botanical celebration. His hand-picked successor, Scottish-born John McLaren, was determined to finish the job – and he was still at it when he died at the age of 93.

Golden Gate Park, a vast green monument to the two dreamers, is filled with anglers, archers, baseball players, cyclists, and enthusiasts of sports, nature, and culture.

The Conservatory of Flowers

natural landscape. The de Young collection includes American art ranging from the 17th to the 20th centuries, as well as art of the Native Americas, Africa, and the Pacific, and a range of textiles and furniture.

Tour buses park near the **Japanese Tea Garden**, a favorite stop on their routes. All the requisite Japanese subtleties are represented at this garden built in 1893 for the Midwinter International Exposition, from rocks among carefully tended shrubs to a koi pond and bridge. Kimono-clad servers pour tea in the outdoor tearoom. Other treasures to be found here include a bronze Buddha from Tajima, Japan, a Zen garden, a *tsukubai*, an ornamental water basin, and a 60ft (18m) tall Buddhist pagoda. 30

Golden Gate Park is also home to a herd of bison, two windmills, an amazing 55-acre (22-hectare) botanical garden, a chain of lakes, a vintage carousel, children's playgrounds, horse stables, tennis and bocce courts, and a polo field.

Richmond and Sunset Districts

31 One of San Francisco's most beautiful museums, the **Palace of the Legion of Honor** (Tue–Sun 9.30am–5.15pm; charge; www.legionofhonor.famsf.org) is located in the city's most northwestern corner, at Lincoln Park in the Richmond District. A collection of 4,000 years of ancient and European art is housed in a Beaux-Arts building in an exquisite setting overlooking the Golden Gate Bridge.

Nearby, set on a dramatic promontory overlooking **Seal Rock**, the haunt of throngs of sea lions and seabirds, the **Cliff House** is a bar and restaurant, with unparalleled ocean views and pricey food (you're paying for the view – worth it on a clear day). Across the road, the eucalyptus, cypress, and pine forests of **Sutro Heights Park** were planted by Adolph Sutro, a German immigrant who became the mayor of San Francisco.

Ocean Beach offers about 4 miles (6km) of inviting sand. Swimming is permitted, though many people opt for wetsuits since the water is extremely cold. Even wading here is dangerous because of the undertow, but sunbathing and sunset-watching remain appealing.

On the landward side of the Great Highway, parallel to Ocean Beach, **San Francisco Zoo** (daily Oct–Apr 9.30am–4pm, May–Sept 9.30am–6pm; charge; www.sfzoo.org), one of the country's older municipal animal parks, underwent renovation and expansion in the 1990s, and continues to update and expand exhibits such as the African Safari, Grizzly Gulch, and the Lemur Forest. Easy 32

Camera Obscura

Perched on cliffs behind the Cliff House, the Camera Obscura, or giant camera, projects a 'live' 360-degree panorama of the nearby Seal Rock into a dark room – it is as eerie an experience today as it was when Leonardo da Vinci invented it back in the 15th century.

San Francisco Zoo

to reach by public transport, the zoo is found at the end of the Muni 'L Taraval' streetcar line. Among the novelties you'll see here are snow leopards, penguins, and koalas.

EXCURSIONS

Within day-trip distance of San Francisco you can experience the most varied scenery and attractions: picturesque harbors, inspiring forests, crashing surf, vineyards as far as the eye can see, and enviable college towns. When is a day trip too grueling? San Francisco excursion companies advertise one-day return tours that go as far as Yosemite National Park – more than 16 hours from start to finish. Lake Tahoe is slightly closer. If you are driving, the wine country north of San Francisco makes a relatively easy day trip, although you may enjoy it more if you take it at a leisurely pace, staying at least one night in a B&B inn for relaxed wine-tasting and gourmet dining.

Here are some ideas for feasible excursions, organized or improvised. We start in the East Bay, move to Marin County, visit Wine Country, and then travel southward to South San Francisco and Monterey.

East Bay

Oakland

If Oakland were just a few hours north from its actual location, it would be a major attraction. But as it stands, in the shadow of San Francisco (that sensational skyline is visible from the Oakland waterfront), it's but a sideshow. How cruel of Gertrude Stein to have written of Oakland, 'There is no there there.' The port city is worth your while, though, and it gives you an excuse to ride the comfortable, fast BART (Bay Area Rapid Transit) line beneath the bay – among the supreme American achievements in public transport. Alternatively, you can drive over the Bay Bridge.

BART deposits you in the City Center shopping zone, with postmodern skyscrapers in view – though Oakland is not really a skyscraper metropolis. 'Old Oakland' has become an entertainment destination in it's own right with Fox and Paramount Theatres being refurbished and attracting top-tier performers from Paul Simon to Elvis Costello to Gogol Bordello. The city has a large amount of parkland; at the centre is **Lake Merritt**, a 155-acre (63-hectare) saltwater lake that has been a game refuge since 1870. It is surrounded by gardens, recreational facilities, and colorful modern apartment and office buildings.

Near the south shore is the low-lying **Oakland Museum of California** (Mon–Fri 10am–4pm, Sat–Sun 10am–5.30pm; charge; www.museumca.org). Set in lushly landscaped architecture, the contents are top-rate and the displays imaginative. The history department, located on the museum's second level, has engrossing exhibits on subjects as old as prehistoric inscriptions and as recent as the beatnik era and beyond. Here you'll find out about how California was born and evolved. The **Gallery of California Art** displays more than 600 revealing works. Starting with the gold rush, newly arrived artists were fascinated by the California sunshine, the people of several races, the drama of Yosemite, and San Francisco Bay.

Jack London 's cabin replica in Oakland

Jack London Square, named in honor of the author who grew up in Oakland, is a shopping, eating, and strolling complex on the shore of the estuary. The seafood restaurants enjoy appetizing views of the busy bay and the San Francisco skyline. For historical interest, a primitive cabin on show here is identified as a replica of the one Jack London lived in when he followed the gold rush to the Yukon. Heinhold's First and Last Chance Saloon, a few steps away, is a London haunt. Just in case you think you've had too much to drink, it's the bar that's tilting; it was salvaged from an old whaler. A floating historic monument is the restored yacht ***Potomac***, moored here, which served as President Franklin Roosevelt's official pleasure craft. After Roosevelt's death, the yacht suffered its ups and downs – Elvis Presley once owned it, and it later sank at Treasure Island.

Berkeley's Campus

Berkeley

Interest focuses not on the city of Berkeley (notable for its bookstores and gourmet restaurants), but on the campus within, a spacious monument to California's drive for academic excellence. If a bright idea really did glow like the light bulb in comic strips, the campus of the **University of California at Berkeley** would look like the Great White Way. With some 30,000 top-flight students and a faculty that includes a galaxy of Nobel Prize-winners, Berkeley can certainly permit itself a swagger of pride and a jot of eccentricity. 33

Start your tour at the **Student Union** building, where a visitor center supplies maps and information. Guided tours of the campus are offered, but you don't really have to wander far from the Union to get the feeling of student life, with all its passions and fashions.

For an excellent vantage point, take the elevator (for a small charge) up **Sather Tower**, otherwise known as the Campanile, which has a 12-bell carillon. It is 307ft (94m) tall and modeled on the one in the Piazza San Marco in Venice. From the top the view puts the town and campus into perspective and offers a superb bird's-eye view of San Francisco, the skyline, and the bay.

Situated just west of the Campanile, the **Bancroft Library** features exhibits of rare books and manuscripts, as well as what's claimed to be the actual nugget that set off the gold rush.

Stadium Rim Road leads to Strawberry Canyon, where you can enjoy roaming the restful yet scientifically significant **Botanical Gardens**. Beyond, the **Lawrence Hall of Science** honors Ernest Lawrence, the first Berkeley professor to win the Nobel Prize (in 1939) and the developer of the cyclotron. The building is more than a physics laboratory; it's a sort of hands-on science fair for children and adults who want to come to grips with the long and the short of science, from astronomy to biology. (Admission is charged.)

The **Hearst Museum of Anthropology** in Kroeber Hall has unusual exhibits on the cultures of several continents. Closer to home, there are artifacts from the last Californian Indian tribesman to come into contact with modern society – Ishi – who eluded the white man until 1911, when he came in from the wild.

Across Bancroft Way, the **Berkeley Art Museum and Pacific Film Archive** (Wed–Sun 11am–5pm, Fri 11am–9pm; charge; www.bampfa.berkeley.edu) has been described as an interpretation of New York's coiled Guggenheim – with corners. Angular spiral ramps are tilted to supersede stairs in a stark concrete interior, which is used to host traveling exhibitions.

Telegraph Avenue and **Peoples' Park** are landmarks of the counter-culture. Here the rebellious children of the protest generation dress more or less as their peacenik parents did when Berkeley spawned the radical

Chef extraordinaire

Champion of locally grown and fresh ingredients in cooking and considered to be creator of 'California cuisine', Alice Waters is a major source of Berkeley pride. Waters's Chez Panisse is located on Shattuck Avenue, and is considered by many to be one of the best, most original restaurants in the world.

Berkeley youth

student movement that swept through the United States in the 1960s, struggling for free speech and against the Vietnam War.

Squatting on the sidewalks, young people today meditate, sell trinkets, tell your fortune, or hand out leaflets about causes they consider just as urgent as their ancestors' crusades. This is still the perfect place to organize an insurrection.

Marin County

Rather than drive, you can take a boat or a public ferry from San Francisco to Sausalito, a half-hour trip. If you drive across the Golden Gate Bridge instead, the views are thrilling, but parking in Sausalito verges on the impossible. During World War II Sausalito prospered, producing Liberty ships on an assembly line. Now one of these abandoned industrial structures houses the San Francisco Bay-Delta Tidal Hydraulic Model, **Bay Model** for short. Covering 1 acre (0.4 hectares), the computerized model simulates the tides. The US Army Corps of Engineers runs tours.

Tiburon, a pleasant harbor town that can be reached by ferryboat, capitalizes on its wonderful views of the San Francisco skyline. In the foreground is **Angel Island**, long used for military purposes but now a state park. At Tiburon's ferry slip is Main Street, a little shopping artery full of character. Follow it around the bend to Ark Row, where you can see pretty houseboats which have been beached and converted into shops.

One of California's most distinguished buildings is visible

from Highway 101 north of San Rafael. The blue-domed **Marin County Civic Center**, a vast hilltop project, was the last work designed by Frank Lloyd Wright. This brilliantly landscaped experiment houses all manner of facilities, from theaters and the county library to the hall of justice.

If you have time for only one brief whiff of the California wilderness, try to make it **Muir Woods National Monument**, just 12 miles (19km) north of the Golden Gate Bridge. The park's 6 miles (10km) of trails offer a sense of tranquillity in the shade of the timeless Coast Redwood trees *(Sequoia sempervirens)*. The aroma of the forest stimulates the lungs and the spirit. The trees – the oldest of which is 1,000 years old – are 250ft (76m) tall and 14ft (4m) thick. The furrows in their bark, like the wrinkles in an old face, seem to attest to all they have survived. The woods were named in honor of the Scottish-born conservationist John Muir (1838–1914) and declared a national monument in 1908 by President Theodore Roosevelt. 34

Redwood giants in the Muir Woods National Monument

35 Another gorgeous spot is the **Point Reyes National Seashore**. The coastline here is so rugged and the surf is so violent that the leaflet and map available at the Bear Valley Visitor Center is full of warnings such as 'Don't go near the water' and 'No life-

In the rolling hills of the Napa Valley

guard on duty.' From December to April, whale-watchers mount the observation platform of the **Point Reyes Lighthouse**, which overlooks a notorious graveyard for ships. The San Andreas Fault, source of all those earthquakes, separates this peninsula from the mainland, and you can visit the **Earthquake Trail**, which points out traces of the 1906 disaster.

Wine Country

The most crowded time to visit the vineyards north of San Francisco is during the grape harvest, in September or October. All year round, however, the beauty of this region is striking, the eating, drinking, and shopping are enjoyable, and the wine-tasting is superb. Here is a glance at what's in store, and where.

Napa Valley

The scenery of America's most famous wine-growing region, Napa County is lovely with rolling hills of grapevines and grazing land, eucalyptus, palms and cedars, and flowers alongside the road. You can tour **Napa Valley** by coach, car, or bicycle, by luxurious vintage train, or from the perspective of a glider or hot-air balloon. 36

The valley begins at the town of **Napa**, with a population of more than 65,000. A neat and pleasant county seat, it is emerging from beneath its blue-collar reputation to become a bonafide destination with a popular marketplace and a refurbished theater that books headlining performers. In the summer and early fall during harvest and on weekends, the hotels fill quickly, as do the more popular restaurants, so advanced reservations are a good idea.

Northward, the small town of **Yountville** moved into big-time tourism when its giant old winery and distillery were converted into a shopping-and-eating complex, Vintage 1870. Among the nearby wineries are the French-run Domaine Chandon, for sparkling wine; Inglenook-Napa Valley, recently acquired by filmmaker and winery owner Francis Ford Coppola; and Beaulieu Vineyards near Rutherford, one of the longest continually producing wineries in the region, founded by George de Latour. Farther afield you'll find the Hess Collection, a Swiss art-lover's contemporary museum and winery.

St Helena is a delightful small town that was smart enough to resist 'progress' – at least on the 1890s-style main street. Just north of town you'll find Beringer Vineyards, founded in 1876, and Christian Brothers, where the monks' traditions are still followed in a stone winery.

Inside a winery

Since the mid-19th century **Calistoga** has been somewhere for 'taking the waters' – and subsequently the wines as well. California's first millionaire, publisher and banker Sam Brannan, bought the land and capitalized on the natural springs. He had planned to name the place Saratoga, after a fashionable spa back east, but during a drinking bout he announced, 'We'll make this place the Calistoga of Sarafornia.' He died in poverty, but Calistoga flourishes with its volcanic ash mudbaths and rejuvenation facilities. When it comes out of the ground the magic water is boiling hot, but it's also bottled and drunk cold – and sold almost everywhere here.

Among the nearby wineries, one of the most unconventional is Clos Pegase, which combines startling postmodern architecture, an art collection, and stylish wines. Like much of the Napa Valley, it's aimed at the trendy well-heeled set.

Closer than Yellowstone National Park, you can see a real **Old Faithful Geyser** (daily winter 9am–5pm, summer 9am–6pm; charge; www.oldfaithfulgeyser.com) just a few miles north of Calistoga. The 60ft (18m) jet of boiling water and vapor shoots out of the ground every 50 minutes.

Let There Be Wine

The Spanish padres who founded missions throughout California were the first to grow grapes here; they needed wine, if only for sacramental purposes. But serious commercial production began in the Sonoma Valley in 1857, thanks to a colorful, wine-loving Hungarian nobleman.

With many varieties of cuttings he imported from Europe, Count Ágoston Haraszthy established the Buena Vista Winery, which is still in operation. He also founded something of an international dynasty. The count's two sons, named Arpad and Attila, married the daughters of the region's Mexican commander, General Mariano Guadalupe Vallejo, simultaneously, at the Sonoma Mission. Count Haraszthy eventually vanished in Nicaragua.

Sonoma Valley

Closer to San Francisco than the Napa Valley, and more relaxed, the Sonoma Valley offers generous helpings of history along with fine wine.

37 **Sonoma**, a captivating town and the county seat, is just how American small towns used to look. Everyone congregates for a chat at the Tuesday evening Farmers' Market in **Sonoma Town Plaza**, which covers an area of 8 acres (3 hectares) – vast even by California standards. It contains the **City Hall**, the tourist office, and a duck pond. History was made here in 1846, as a monument in the square recounts, when the flag of the California Republic was first raised. This was a grass-roots American revolt against Mexican rule, which was overtaken by events less than a month later. The Bear Flag is now the official flag of the state of California. Northeast of the plaza, the San Francisco **Solano Mission**, founded in 1823, is the northernmost of the 21 Californian missions. The paintings in the adobe church were done by Indian parishioners.

The historic City Hall in Sonoma Town Plaza

Other buildings around the square include a Mexican army barracks, 19th-century hotels, and historic homes which are now shops and restaurants. Nearby is the house built by General Vallejo, Victorian-Gingerbread in style, and quite possibly the most un-Mexican house in the whole of California. He called it 'Lachryma Montis,' the Latin translation of the original Indian name for this area – 'crying mountain.'

The wine trail starts within the Sonoma city limits. The Sebastiani Vineyards, producing everything from serious vintages to jugs of popular wines, have tours and tastings. Just outside town is Buena Vista, which maintains a tasting room at 18000 Old Winery Road. Ravenswood, known for producing 'big reds' like Zinfandel, at 18701 Gehricke Road, offers tours, tastings, and barbecues. Quirky Gundlach Bundschu winery is a fun place to visit and known for world-class Cabernet wines.

South of San Francisco

Two main highways run southeastward down the San Francisco Peninsula. Interstate 101, linking the city with the airport, can be as jammed and intimidating as one of the Los Angeles freeways. Somewhat less stressful, and definitely more picturesque, is Interstate Highway 280 (or the Junípero Serra Freeway), with a scenery bonus of dramatic mountainous countryside.

Just by the Edgewood Road exit of I-280, you can visit the stately home of **Filoli**, with 16 acres (6.5 hectares) of formal gardens. 'Filoli' may sound Italian, but it's an acronym for Fight, Love, Live. It was the motto of the owner of the estate, William Bourn, who inherited a gold-rush fortune and parlayed it to even greater wealth as owner of San Francisco's water supply and the head of the gas company. The gardens have something in bloom most of the year.

Founded in 1885 by the railroad tycoon Leland Stanford, **Stanford University** occupies a dream campus so vast you need a bus, a bike, or a car to get around. It covers 8,180 acres (3,310 hectares) from the Santa Clara Valley to the foothills of the Santa Cruz Mountains. An avenue of stately palms leads from town to the center of campus, the cloistered Main Quadrangle, whose architecture is described as a mixture of Romanesque and Mission Revival. The tallest and most striking building on campus, the **Hoover Tower**, honors an alumnus, US President Herbert Hoover. The tower and neighboring buildings house the Hoover Institution on War, Revolution and Peace, where great political thinkers have researched and deliberated. From the top of the tower you can see the expanse of Mediterranean-style tile roofs that begins on the campus and stretches out as far as the sea.

Admirers of beautiful college campuses should continue from Silicon Valley to **Santa Cruz**, where a redwood forest hides the Santa Cruz division of the state-run University of California system. For its landscape and modern architecture, UCSC, which opened in 1966, is a dynamic endeavor. But there's more than intellectual activity hereabouts. The city of Santa Cruz itself, down the hill, has a 1-mile (1.6km) long swimming beach and an old-fashioned boardwalk with vintage amusement park.

The Hoover Tower at Stanford

Monterey Peninsula

A scenic two-hour drive south of San Francisco brings you to the Monterey Peninsula, a happy convergence of history, charm, and some of the world's most astounding seascapes. Thanks to the work of conservationists, lobbyists, and far-sighted politicians, the sea lions and seabirds enjoy an unthreatened life along the cliffs and beaches, cypress forests thrive on the ocean breezes, and the towns remain eminently desirable.

38 The peninsula's principal city, **Monterey**, was the capital of Spanish, Mexican, and briefly, American California, until the gold rush shifted attention to Sacramento. The hilltop **Presidio** of Monterey, the first of the Spanish fortresses founded in California, serves to this day as a United States Army base – the home of the Defense Language Institute, where military interpreters are trained. Also in Monterey is another elite military institution, the US Naval Postgraduate School.

Inside the Monterey Bay Aquarium

Crowds of vacationers spend time on **Fisherman's Wharf**, with its cheery boardwalk atmosphere, seafood restaurants, and souvenir shops. Bay sightseeing boats, whale-watching tours (from mid-December until March), and deep-sea fishing expeditions all leave from here. Note the adobe **Custom House**, built in 1814. It was here that the American flag was first raised in California, in 1846.

Legend leads most visitors to Monterey's **Cannery Row**, immortalized by John Steinbeck in his 1945 novel of the same name. However, it has all been spruced up and rather fictionalized since those noisy, smelly, eccentric days. The derelict sardine canneries and related structures have been regenerated for the tourism business, and are now art galleries, shopping malls, amusements, and even a wax museum featuring characters from Steinbeck's novels.

The top tourist attraction in town is the **Monterey Bay Aquarium** (May–Sept 9.30am–6pm, Sept–May 10am–6pm; charge; www.mbayaq.org). Many millions of dollars and all the best ideas in aquarium design and presentation were channeled into this institution, which was inaugurated in 1984. There are light-hearted explanations of all the phenomena of the sea, which mainly focus on the rich local scene. Monterey Canyon, just offshore, is the undersea equivalent of Arizona's Grand Canyon – it's nearly 2 miles (3km) deep! Children of all ages will enjoy the 'touching pool,' which includes bat rays, a type of stingray (but they don't sting). Meanwhile, delightful sea otters frolic both inside and outside the aquarium.

The little-frequented town of **Pacific Grove**, founded by Methodists in 1875, has a fine collection of Victorian cottages and a very beautiful public golf course. In addition, gulls, pelicans, cormorants, and other seabirds in transit traverse the lovely coastline, and millions of Monarch butterflies winter here.

Seventeen-Mile Drive is so spectacular that people pay to see what lies beyond the toll booth. This is also California's golf capital, home of the exclusive Pebble Beach course.

Luxury typifies the small town of **Carmel-by-the-Sea**, once a bohemian playground now a sleepy bedroom community that belongs to the very rich. Here you'll find a tremendous range of art galleries, boutiques, and fashionable restaurants. At the end of the main street's incline, a seemingly endless beach of white sand begins. Carmel's 18th-century mission was the favorite of the mission system's founder, Father Junípero Serra, who is buried here.

WHAT TO DO

San Francisco's mild climate, cultural sophistication and adventurous spirit make for a wealth of choices when it comes to leisure time. Outdoor activities can be enjoyed year round, the diversity of cultures add an international flair to events and festivals, and San Francisco's position as a world-class city is evidenced by top-shelf theater, arts, music, and shopping.

ENTERTAINMENT

From opera and avant-garde theater to seedy strip shows, clangorous alternative music clubs, or languorous cocktail lounges, every aspect of entertainment is available in San Francisco. Particular kinds of entertainments seem to cluster in neighborhoods: Try Nob Hill for a sentimental piano bar, North Beach for the blues or jazz, Union Square for theater, SoMa for dance clubs, Civic Center for culture. In addition, you will find congenial haunts with singular ethnic, musical, or social orientation spread all over town.

For a preview of coming attractions, study newspaper websites, such as www.sfgate.com/eguide, www.sfweekly.com, www.sfstation.com, www.sfbg.com, or the city guide www.bayarea.citysearch.com. Once in town, consult the edetailed survey of what's on in the 'Datebook' section of the Sunday edition of the *San Francisco Chronicle*, or study a copy of either *SF Weekly* or the *Bay Guardian*, a giveaway weekly easily found in bookstores, cafés, and in sidewalk kiosks.

If too much pre-planning removes all the excitement of an evening out, meander down to the TIX counter (tel: 415-433-7827; www.tixbayarea.com) on the west side of Union Square.

Neon lights of San Fran

Here, tickets for certain shows are available at half price, starting at 11am on the day of the performance only. (TIX also sells full-price tickets for future performances. It's closed Monday.)

Opera, Ballet, Classical Music

War Memorial Opera House (Van Ness Avenue at Grove Street), in the shadow of City Hall, is one of the most glamorous venues for an evening out. The gala season of the San Francisco Opera Company (tel: 415-864-3330) runs from September to December, followed by a season of the San Francisco Ballet (tel: 415-865-2000) on the same stage from February until June (the exact dates of these seasons vary slightly each year, so check in advance). Across the street from the Opera House is **Davies Symphony Hall**, where the San Francisco Symphony Orchestra (tel: 415-864-6000) holds forth between September and July.

Theater and Cinema

Among dozens of theater groups, the **American Conservatory Theater** (415 Geary Street, tel: 415-749-2228) has acquired the widest national reputation. Its repertory season runs from October until June. Broadway hits appear next door at the **Curran Theater** or, a few blocks away, the **Golden Gate Theater** and **Orpheum**. All three venues share the same telephone number (tel: 415-551-2000). In summer there's free Shakespeare in Golden Gate Park.

As far as the cinema is concerned, there are multiplexes along Van Ness Avenue, in Japantown, at the Embarcadero Center, and South of Market at Westfield San Francisco Centre, and the Metreon. The Roxie in the Mission District is a popular art-house movie theater. The Castro Theater, a movie palace built in the 1920s on Castro Street, is often the spot for interesting documentaries, cult films, sing-a-longs, and film-festival favorites.

Clubs and Bars

Night owls looking to step out on the town have no shortage of possibilities.

Head to North Beach for stalwart bars like **Vesuvio** (255 Columbus Avenue, tel: 415-362-3370, www.vesuvio.com), where Jack Kerouac tipped back pints or catch a glimpse of local celebrities at **Tosca** (242 Columbus Avenue, tel: 415-986-9651, www.toscacafesf.com).

The funky, diverse Mission is hipster heaven – from biker bar **Zeitgeist** (199 Valencia Street, tel: 415-255-7505, www.zeitgeist.com) with an outdoor beer garden to **Little Baobab** (3388 19th Street, tel: 415-643-3558, www.bissapbaobab.com) for DJ dance parties with an international flair.

Haight Street contains a trove of nightspots. **Toronado** (547 Haight Street, tel: 415-863-2276, www.toronado.com) is a beer drinker's paradise, while more highbrow options

Vesuvio is a North Beach favorite

include the stylish **Aub Zam Zam** (1633 Haight Street, tel: 415-861-2545) and swanky **Alembic** (1725 Haight Street, tel: 415-666-0822, www.alembicbar.com).

Rock out at one of many music venues including the legendary **Fillmore** (1805 Geary Boulevard, tel: 415-346-3000, www.thefillmore.com), 1950s throwback **Bimbo's** (1025 Columbus Avenue, www.bimbos365club.com, tel: 415-474-0365); bordello chic **Great American Music Hall** (859 O'Farrell Street, tel: 415-885-0750, www.gamh.com), groovy, eclectic **Independent** (628 Divisidero Street, tel: 415-771-1421, www.theindependentsf.com), the **Boom Boom Room** blues club (1601 Fillmore Street, tel: 415-673-8000, www.boomboomblues.com), **Yoshi's** jazz club (1330 Fillmore Street, tel: 415-655-5600, www.yoshis.com), and **Café du Nord** (2170 Market Street, tel: 415-861-5016, www.cafedunord.com).

The Castro has the largest concentration of gay bars including **The Café** (2369 Market Street, tel: 415-834-5840, www.cafesf.com) and **Q Bar** (456 Castro Street, tel: 415-864-2877, www.qbarsf.com). Two of the best-known lesbian hangouts include the **Lexington Club** (2464 19th Street, tel: 415-863-2052, www.lexingtonclub.com) and **Wild Side West** (424 Cortland Avenue, tel: 415-647-3099).

Laidback drinking spots on the waterfront include **Pier 23 Café** (Pier 23, tel: 415-362-5125, www.pier23cafe.com) and at **The Ramp** (855 Terry Francois Street, tel: 415-621-2378, www.therамprestaurant.com).

For the dance partiers, SoMa is the big draw. Check

Historic venue

The legendary Fillmore Auditorium was the incubator of the San Francisco sound in the '60s, where event producer Bill Graham launched his empire, and Jefferson Airplane, the Grateful Dead, and Janis Joplin 'made the scene.' Intimate, historic and filled with photos and posters, it remains one of the city's best music venues.

Having fun at an open-air club in San Francisco

out **DNA Lounge** (375 Eleventh Street, tel: 415-626-1409, www.dnalounge.com), and **Temple** (540 Howard Street, tel: 415-978-9942, www.templesf.com).

Comedy and Cabaret

Cobb's Comedy Club (tel: 415-928-4320; www.cobbs comedyclub.com) and the **Purple Onion** (tel: 415-956-1653; www.caffemacaroni.com) are both good venues in North Beach. **The Punchline** (444 Battery Street; tel: 415-397-7573; www.punchlinecomedyclub.com) hosts national and local talent nightly. For cabaret and jazz vocalists check out the **Rrazz Room** at the Hotel Nikko (tel: 415-394-1181; www.therrazzroom.com). In North Beach, a gloriously silly musical review, *Beach Blanket Babylon*, has packed in audiences for over two decades; adults only except for Sunday matinees. Buy tickets well in advance for these popular shows; tel: 415-421-4222; www.beachblanketbabylon.com.

SHOPPING

Like the city itself, shopping in San Francisco is stylish, cosmopolitan, and innovative. Here you will find whatever you've been looking for, including fashions, trends, and gadgets you never knew you needed.

Where to Shop

The place to start for a survey of San Francisco shopping is **Union Square**. The department stores are here, along with elegant boutiques down the nearby lanes. Also downtown is the **Westfield San Francisco Shopping Centre** that spans most of the block on Fifth Street between Market and Mission streets and includes hundreds of stores, including Nordstrom and Bloomingdale's, as well as an array of dining options.

Record store in North Beach

SoMa (South of Market) holds treasures in fashion, funky furniture, and home decor. Discount outlets also abound in the neighborhood.

Historic **Jackson Square**, on the edge of the Financial District, specializes in pricey antiques sold in old brick Barbary Coast surroundings.

Chinatown is a seething bazaar, where the choice of exotica is overwhelming – from an abacus to fortune cookies.

The **Embarcadero Center** – like Chinatown, another city-within-the-city – is an urban redevelopment project similar in scale to the Rockefeller Plaza in New York, with more than 150 shops among the offices, restaurants, cafés, sculptures, and bright flower-filled pots.

North Beach, birthplace of the beatniks, specializes in offbeat shops, boutiques, and the famous City Lights bookstore. Also eccentric is **Haight Street**, the main thoroughfare of the one-time flower-power Haight-Ashbury District, with lots of funky clothing stores, thrift and vintage stores, and head shops.

Union Street, an area of Victorian-era houses, is now a smart shopping zone of stylish boutiques, accessories for home and body, and lots of restaurants. Same for **Fillmore Street** and **Chestnut Street**, which contains some only-in-San-Francisco gems.

Fisherman's Wharf is geared toward tourists, with sweatshirt emporia, mass-produced souvenirs, and sometimes cheesy art that lines Jefferson Street and spills into **Pier 39**. A better choice is **Ghirardelli Square**, a 19th-century factory complex overlooking the bay, which has been converted into a tasteful array of shops, galleries, and restaurants. **The Cannery** also has three floors of shops, cafés, and attractions in an 1890s former peach cannery across the street.

What to Buy

San Francisco is a great place to shop for art, high-quality crafts, clothing, items for the home, and wine. Be sure to browse offbeat galleries and gift shops where many local artists provide everything from funky jewelry and handbags fashioned from antique kimonos to hand-painted furniture.

Books. San Francisco has a long publishing tradition, and independent bookstores abound. Some of the best are City Lights (North Beach), Green Apple (Clement Street in the Richmond district), the Booksmith (Haight), Books, Inc.

(Chestnut Street and Laurel Village) and Modern Times (Mission). Many bookstores host special literary events.

Clothing. Sportswear and casual styles are the best bet. Blue jeans fans should check out the Levi's store on Union Square. For unique local designer clothing, jewelry, handbags, and other apparel, you'll find lots of small and stylish boutiques on the east side of Columbus near Grant Avenue in North Beach, upper Fillmore Street in Pacific Heights Union Street in Cow Hollow, Hayes Street in Hayes Valley, and Haight Street.

Food and drink. The Ferry Building downtown hosts farmers' markets three times weekly outside and boasts a range of specialty food shops and high-end artisan grocers within. Other farmers' markets pop up on different days in different locations around the city. For a list, visit http://events.sfgate.com/san-francisco-ca/events/farmers+markets. Chinatown and Clement Street are both troves for hard-to-find Asian ingredients, Chinese herbs, and inexpensive cookware and dishes.

There are a number of good wine shops, including the Jug Shop on Polk Street, Coit Liquors in North Beach, Cask on Market and Third Street, and the Wine Club in SoMa.

Sourdough bread is wrapped 'to go' at the airport – handy if you've a long wait. Also, San Francisco chocolates, candies, and salami make good portable souvenirs. Or why not take home a bottle of fine California wine?

The home team

There are a few Giants dugout stores, one right at the ballpark on Willie Mays Plaza. The shops sell Major League Baseball-sanctioned goods, including sweatshirts, caps, and other Giants paraphernalia.

Gadgets. The bustling Apple Store on Market Street offers lots of eye candy for those looking at the latest innovations from Apple. A multitude of workstations are wired up for you to jump on and check out the goods.

If you're in need of electronic goods, recording devices, wires, batteries, etc, there are several Radio Shack locations in the city, including one on Market Street and two locations of Best Buy will satisfy those in need of electronics and appliances large and small.

Noe Valley toy store

Toys. Kids Only on Haight Street is small and pricey but has lots of unique gifts and toys for little ones. Noe Valley and Sacramento Street in Presidio Heights are both havens for children and both have outposts of the Ark, with a fine selection of wooden toys. City Kids on Clement is another excellent choice.

Head Shops. The Haight is known for its 'head shops,' and while there are far fewer than even a couple of decades ago, you will still find psychedelic posters, rock T-shirts, stickers with anti-establishment messages, and drug paraphernalia.

Cosmetics. Stop into Benefit Cosmetics on Fillmore or Chestnut Street for a quick pick-me-up – you can get waxed, have a brow tint, or even a free makeover with your purchase. Sephora on Powell Street also has a dizzying array of cosmetic lines.

Art and Antiques. Union Square is gallery central, and the building at 49 Geary hosts 'first Thursday' – a monthly showcase of (mostly) local art – the place to see, be seen, and buy art. You'll also find a number of galleries in the SoMa and Mission districts, and sprinkled throughout the city. In the Parisian-looking enclave of Jackson Square, the antiques business thrives.

ACTIVE PURSUITS

Never too hot, never too cool, the climate encourages sporting people of many disciplines to excel year round. Only the swimming can be problematic. The beaches may be beautiful, but the tides are treacherous, the water cold, and the fog can cast a pall. Consider a wetsuit before you decide to take a dip.

Cycling

Yet another San Francisco advantage, with all the scenic surroundings available. Two good bike routes, one through Golden Gate Park to the Great Highway, another from the southern part of the city to the Golden Gate Bridge, are a good way to get acquainted with the city. Rental shops are to be found alongside the park, in North Beach and in Fishermans Wharf. For rules of the road, city bike lanes, maps, and routes, visit http://bicycling.511.org or www.sfbike.org.

Jogging

Golden Gate Park is a favorite, but you might like to experience the 5-mile (8km) path around Lake Merced, or the bay views from the Marina Green and Crissy Field, or parallel the Pacific on Ocean Beach. Running along the Embarcadero from China Basin to the Presidio is another popular course. Serious runners can compete in the San Francisco Marathon, or the costume-optional Bay to Breakers Run.

Sponsored walks

Sponsored by the San Francisco Public Library, City Guides offer free historical and architectural walking tours 52 weeks a year, rain or shine. Among the 30 offerings are Art Deco Marina, City Hall Ghost Walk, Bawdy & Naughty, 1906 Earthquake, and Fire, and Russian Hill Stairways.

Cycling is a great way to get around

Hiking

There are many beautiful hiking trails on Mt Tamalpais across the bay in Marin, but you don't have to leave the city to break in your boots. For views and a challenging walk, take the **Coastal Trail** from Fort Point (underneath the Golden Gate Bridge) to the Cliff House; but don't climb on the cliffs themselves, as they aren't stable. Eight miles from the shore, **Angel Island** sports a dozen miles of trails; ride the Blue and Gold Ferry and take a picnic lunch. Within the city, climb Buena Vista Park, Mount Davidson, Tank Hill, Corona Heights, Strawberry Hill in Golden Gate Park or scale Bernal Heights for awe-inspiring views.

Boating

For bay boating, with or without a licensed captain, see the charter firms along The Embarcadero or in Sausalito. The Blue and Gold fleet (tel: 415-773-1188) offers one-hour bay cruises that pass under the Golden Gate Bridge and around Alcatraz and Angel islands. Other companies that combine dining with sailing and water activities and adventures, include The Ruby (tel: 415-861-2165), and Hornblower Cruises and Events (tel: 415-788-8866; www.hornblower.com). Hornblower also offers cruises to Alcatraz.

Fishing

Several deep-sea fishing companies operate out of Fisherman's Wharf. Boats leave early in the morning in search of salmon, bass, or whatever is running.

Golf

There are six public courses, including the 18-hole Presidio green opened to the public in 1995 (tel: 415-561-4653). For golf as well as inspiring views, try out the Lincoln Park (www.parks.sfgov.org or Harding Park (tel: 415-664-4690) courses. If you've come to California for the golfing experience of your life, Pebble Beach is less than three hours by car south of San Francisco.

On the Beaches

If you don't mind brisk temperatures, go ahead and dip your toes in the Pacific Ocean. Here are some sandy beaches, reading from north to south:

Baker Beach, part of the Presidio, is highly unsafe for swimming but popular with joggers, picnickers, and sunbathers (nude ones on the northern portion).

China Beach is a protected cove where swimming is permitted.

Ocean Beach runs on and on alongside the Great Highway south from the Cliff House. Swimming can be quite dangerous, but the sand and sunsets are superb.

Tennis

AT&T Park, home to the San Francisco Giants

There are over 100 well-maintained tennis courts in parks around San Francisco that are city-run and free – first come, first served. (The courts at Dolores Park on Dolores and 18th Street are lit at night.) A fee is charged for the 21 courts in Golden Gate Park. At the top end of the market, the San Francisco Tennis Club at 645 Fifth Street (tel: 415-777-9000) has indoor and outdoor courts as well as exercise facilities.

Spectator Sports

Baseball. One of the great American pastimes unfolds at the fantastic AT&T Park, when the 2010 World Champion San Francisco Giants are in town. Seating is limited to 40,000, so tickets may be difficult to come by but there are vantage points to watch games for free. Across the bridge, the A's play at the Coliseum in Oakland.

Basketball. Big-time basketball takes over after the baseball season ends. The Golden State Warriors of the National Basketball Association's Pacific Division entertain in Oakland's Network Associates Coliseum.

Football. Named after the gold-rush invaders, the powerful San Francisco '49ers of the National Football League are based at Candlestick Park. The season runs from August to December. Tickets are nearly impossible to get.

Horse racing. The nearest thoroughbred racing is held at Golden Gate Fields (tel: 510-559-7300) in Albany, north of Berkeley off Interstate 80.

CHILDREN'S SAN FRANCISCO

There are a number of exciting museums that will do the trick without raising resistance from the kids. For example, the made-for-children **Exploratorium** is one of the world's finest science museums, and full of hands-on exhibits to suit all ages.

In Golden Gate Park, the amazing **California Academy of Sciences** is an architectural masterpiece with an actual 'living roof,' a mesmerizing underground aquarium, and a three-story rainforest exhibit that will engage children and adults alike. There is also an acclaimed café and restaurant within. **Zeum** at Yerba Buena Gardens is a fascinating technology center geared toward older kids and teenagers with an interest in computers, art, and video. Nearby on Fourth Street is the **Cartoon Art Museum**, with exhibits on underground and mainstream comics.

Ice-skating and **bowling** are other favorites at Yerba Buena Gardens. **The Metreon** is a kid magnet and renowned for its IMAX theater, the largest 3D screen in the world. Farther afield, **San Francisco Zoo** is home to over 1,000 animals and also features a zoo train and a large playground. Down near **Fisherman's Wharf** and **Aquatic Park** are seaworthy places to spend time with the kids, including the **Hyde Street Pier**, home to historic ships open for tours and the **Aquarium of the Bay** is located at Pier 39. The **Musée Mécanique** is loaded with restored mechanical toys and games that were the forerunners to pinball and video machines.

Having fun at Zeum

Festivals

Parades, street fairs, and celebrations of the most exotic types occur with great frequency in San Francisco. Some of the highlights to note are:

February–March: Chinese New Year: fireworks, dragon dances, and a parade through Chinatown. St Patrick's Day parade, downtown.

April: Cherry Blossom Festival, Japantown. SF International Film Festival, various locations around town.

May: Cinco de Mayo (May 5) Mexican fiesta and parade, Mission District. Carnaval Festival (Memorial Day weekend), Mission District: a wild parade and festival featuring samba dancers, food, crafts, music. Bay to Breakers, on the third Sunday in May, is like no other 12K on the planet. Runners, walkers, and partiers don wild costumes and meander the 7½ miles from downtown SF to Ocean Beach.

June: Gay Pride parade to the Civic Center. Union Street Fair, arts and crafts on Union between Fillmore and Gough Streets. North Beach Festival, the oldest urban street fair.

July: Fourth of July fireworks along the waterfront. Jazz and All That Art on Fillmore, Fillmore Street between Post and Jackson streets. San Francisco Marathon, one of the largest marathons in the world.

September: Shakespeare Festival in the Presidio's Main Post. Sausalito Art Festival, an impressive showcase of art combined with international wine and food and solid musical performances. Autumn Moon Festival in Chinatown. Festival de las Américas, Mission District.

October: Columbus Day parade, Italian-American Festival in North Beach. Castro Street Fair. Exotic-Erotic Ball on Halloween. Jazz Festival. Hardly Strictly Bluegrass Festival, three days of free music in Golden Gate Park. Fleet Week, which includes aerial performances of the Blue Angels, a US Navy and Marine demonstration pilot squad.

November: Burning Man, on Labor Day weekend hordes of San Franciscans join others from all over the globe to head to the Black Rock Desert in Nevada, where they build a temporary city filled with massive art installations and burn a 50ft (15m) tall wooden man. Day of the Dead Festival, Mission District. Bay Area Book Festival, Fort Mason.

EATING OUT

The success of the San Francisco food scene can be summed up in just one word: abundance. Over 5,000 eating and drinking establishments, said to be more per capita than anywhere else in the world, exploit a cornucopia of natural ingredients fresh from the sea and California's rich farming zones. Local gourmets have developed high expectations, which inspire ever greater achievements from the chefs, some of whom are internationally renowned.

Thanks to its Pacific outlook and long-established ethnic communities, the city has always offered a prolific array of cuisines. The city claims to have opened the first pizzeria in America and the first Chinese and Japanese restaurants in the West. Visitors can sample and purchase cracked Dungeness crab and fresh petrale sole from the dockside stands of Fisherman's Wharf; Italian gnocchi and oven-fresh focaccia bread from the tiny storefronts of North Beach; armsful of French bread; warm tortillas and chili-laden salsas from the Mexican-influenced Mission; and Thai fish cakes and Chinese pot stickers from Clement Street, deep in the heart of the Richmond District.

But where San Francisco really comes into its own is California cuisine. This eclectic culinary style resulted from a rebellion against the

Meals on wheels

Food trucks like Curry Up Now, pedaling Indian street food, and Chairman Bao, serving Asian steamed buns, are part of a foodie trend that brings global street food to urban eaters in a carnival-like atmosphere. Off the Grid (www.offthegridsf.com) organizes weekly events in the Haight, Chinatown, Mission, and Civic Center, but the ultimate mobile gastronomic event is held at Fort Mason on Friday evenings.

convention that French food belonged in French restaurants, Chinese in Chinese restaurants, and so on. Experimentation and the mixing and melding of international ingredients – along with a decidedly Western touch – gave rise to a revolution.

Taylor's Automatic Refresher

At the centre of this revolution was Alice Waters's Chez Panisse *(see page 71)*, which opened in Berkeley in 1971. Waters made the freshness and quality of ingredients her top priority, and began encouraging local purveyors to bring produce to her kitchen door. This fervor for freshness chimed with the Californian ethos and helped jump-start the move to organic farming. Now, small local producers of everything from heirloom tomatoes and baby lettuces to olive oil and free-range chickens deliver to the back doors of small and large establishments, whose menus vary depending on what's in season.

The revamped Ferry Building is a great place to sample some of the best food San Francisco has to offer. The old warehouse interior has been transformed into a hugely popular artisan food and wares market and high-end eating destination, where everything is locally grown and produced. You can choose from handcrafted chocolates, caviar dishes, oysters from Hog Island (in Tomales Bay), and cheeses from the Cowgirl Creamery.

When to Eat

Small-town Americans have dinner as early as 5pm, even when they come to San Francisco, but it's more fashionable to dine after 7pm, and most restaurants stay open to 10pm or later. Phone ahead for dinner reservations. Breakfast is served from about 7am to about 10am, though in some places breakfast dishes such as pancakes and scrambled eggs are served throughout the day. Lunch is usually served between noon and 2pm.

Specialties

The big draw in San Francisco is the **seafood**, so wholesome that it doesn't take a famous chef to do it justice. **Dungeness Crab** is the local specialty. It is available from mid-November to May and is served in many forms – steamed, cracked and dunked in butter, au gratin, or, less elegantly, as morsels in takeaway plastic cups.

For an unusual take on a classic seafood dish, try San Francisco-style **clam chowder**, which is served in sourdough-bread bowls on Fisherman's Wharf.

One part-seafood dish even comes with its own legend. The wryly named **Hangtown Fry** – scrambled eggs, ham, and

By Bread Alone

You'd have to go to Paris to find a bread remotely as tasty as San Francisco's sourdough. Many tourists carry home souvenir loaves.

What makes sourdough bread so good is the secret ingredient, descended from a micro-organism brought from Europe in time for the gold rush. Prospectors carried small quantities of fermented dough, or 'starter', to mix with the bread they baked in the wilds to make it rise. A bit of this starter is recycled every day in the complex process used by the bakeries of San Francisco. Sourer or sweeter, darker or lighter, according to your choice, the crusty end product can be a meal in itself.

oysters – is said to have been devised in gold-rush days by a gallows-bound prisoner. For his last meal, the wily criminal requested ingredients that would take some time to assemble.

Carnivores will enjoy SF cuisine

Seafood also figures in many of the ethnic restaurants. **Cioppino**, an Italian-descended seafood stew, is claimed as a San Francisco original. Thai restaurants serve spicy crab salad, Chinese chefs immerse lobster in black-bean sauce, and fresh scallops and prawns appear in Japanese sushi.

Fresh fish from the Pacific, such as swordfish, salmon, and tuna, also appears on many menus.

Meat eaters can start with steaks in their all-American diversity – Porterhouse, filet mignon, T-bone. Roast beef, veal, lamb, and pork round out the menu. In the meantime, don't underestimate the great American hamburger.

For **vegetarians** California offers a better choice than almost anywhere else in the States. Not only are the ingredients impeccable, but there's an understanding of nutritional requirements. There are plenty of vegetarian eateries in town, and a few achieve gourmet level; almost all local restaurants have creative vegetarian dishes on the menu.

Desserts include some delicious, locally grown fresh fruits. Pies and cakes are as rich as you can stand them, and the ice cream, in a truly bewildering array of flavors, is sensational. Some upscale restaurants have cheeses on the dessert menu, although the list is growing.

Californian grapes

California Wine

California's wine makers have added the advantages of science and technology to an already blessed climate, assuring consistently excellent results. Scientists at the University of California at Davis have bred hybrid grapes, designed to upgrade hitherto boring table wines. Visiting wine aficionados will enjoy tracking down world-class vintages. To the ordinary diner, the California wine revolution simply means that even the lowest price house wine on the menu is eminently drinkable.

Every sort of wine produced in Europe has its equivalent in California – plus Japanese *sake*, distilled from local rice and served in sushi bars and Japanese restaurants.

Labels identify the winery, region, variety of grape, vintage year if appropriate, and alcoholic content. Classic grapes like Cabernet Sauvignon and Pinot Noir are represented, along with less familiar hybrids like Gamay Beaujolais. California's vineyards stretch from San Diego County, where the Spanish friars planted the first grapes in 1769, to Mendocino in the cool north. You don't have to be an expert in varietals and vintages to enjoy forays in the Sonoma and Napa valleys, the wine zones most easily accessible from San Francisco *(see pages 74–8)*. Take advantage of the tastings and tours offered by many of the popular wineries.

Other Drinks

In cosmopolitan San Francisco people drink Scotch whisky or various types of vodka, sometimes infused with fruit or other flavorings, Irish coffee or Mexican tequila, as well as a staggering range of **cocktails**. One of the most well-known perhaps is a **margarita** – iced tequila with Cointreau or Triple Sec, lime juice, and a coating of salt around the rim of the glass.

Beer, domestic or imported, is normally served very cold. There are 'micro-breweries' all over town, where you can admire the gleaming tanks and taste various styles of beer and ale produced on the premises. San Francisco's contribution to the science of beer-making is 'steam beer,' a historic method of brewing using air-cooling rather than ice.

Coffee is extremely popular, as evidenced by the enormous amount of real estate taken up with coffee shops.

Juice bars offer **fruit juices** with a scoop of protein powder and **smoothies** – fresh juices mixed with yogurt, ice and sometimes vitamins, herbs or wheat grass, often replace meals.

Brewery tours

Beer-lovers will enjoy a trip to the Anchor Steam Brewery for a tour and tasting. Tours are free and conducted once a week, by reservation only (tel: 415-863-8350). Book as early in advance as possible for the two-hour tour followed by a tasting of the classic beer.

PLACES TO EAT

We have used the following symbols to give an idea of the price for a three-course meal for one without wine. Remember that taxes (8.5 percent) and tips (around 20 percent) will increase your bill:

$$$ over $40 **$$** $20–40 **$** below $20

CHINATOWN

House of Nanking $ *919 Kearny Street, tel: 415-421-1429.* Open for lunch and dinner daily. Grungy, crowded, and not particularly clean, the reason for the lengthy line at nearly all hours is because this wildly popular spot, a locals' favorite, serves outstanding, inexpensive, adventurous Chinese food. The no-nonsense owners/staff will tell you what's good tonight. Listen to them. Lunch specials are even more affordable, with large portions. Beware – service is terse and rushed.

Kay Cheung $ *615 Jackson Street, tel: 415-989-6838.* Open daily for dim sum, lunch, and dinner. This small, pleasant dining room serves delicious Hong Kong-style Chinese dishes at a great price. Offers an interesting selection of fresh seafood (plucked live from tanks) and dim sum. If you end up sharing a table, take an opportunity to learn about dumplings from the Chinatown regulars who come here between their shopping excursions.

R&G Lounge $ *631 Kearny Street, tel: 415-982-7877.* Open for lunch and dinner daily. Downstairs you'll find excellent Hong Kong Chinese food served in a drab setting by bored-looking waiters. The upstairs dining room is much more comfortable, with attentive servers who can help design your meal. No matter where they seat you, don't pass up the signature salt and pepper crab.

UNION SQUARE

Le Colonial $$$ *20 Cosmo Place, tel: 415-931-3600.* Open for dinner nightly. Le Colonial offers flavorful French-Vietnamese food in the lush, romantic surroundings of a dining room that is replete with rattan, pressed tin, potted palms, and ceiling fans. The upstairs lounge and outside veranda area is a great place for a delicious tropical drink and an appetizer.

Dottie's True Blue Café $ *522 Jones Street, tel: 415-885-2767.* Open for breakfast and lunch Wednesday through Monday only. If you like a big breakfast featuring fresh baked goods, pancakes, omelets, and maybe a pork chop, get in line for one of the 11 tables packed into this tiny place. Lunch isn't quite as crowded, but it's equally good.

Grand Café $–$$$ *501 Geary Street, tel: 415-292-0101.* Open daily for breakfast, brunch, lunch, and dinner. There's always a buzz of activity at this soaring and stylish restaurant inside Hotel Monaco that serves contemporary French-California cuisine in a renovated turn-of-the-century ballroom. It's a destination for tourists as well as locals looking for a major meal or just an after-theater bite to eat. Roasts, fresh fish, brick-oven pizzas, big desserts – every plate receives careful attention from the kitchen.

Scala's Bistro $$–$$$ *432 Powell Street, tel: 415-395-8555.* Open daily for breakfast, lunch, and dinner. Next to the Sir Francis Drake hotel, this Italian restaurant has a broad menu, comfortable booths, and a warm, clubby atmosphere. Highlights of the menu include a terrific Caesar salad, creative pastas, well-prepared fish dishes, and an extensive wine list featuring Californian and Italian wines.

Shalimar $ *532 Jones Street, tel: 415-928-0333.* Consistently rated one of the best restaurants in the city, this spot serves traditional and tasty Indian and Pakistani food every day for lunch and dinner. No alcohol. Cash only.

NOB HILL

Nob Hill Café $$–$$$ *1152 Taylor Street, tel: 415-776-6500.* Open for lunch and dinner daily, Saturday and Sunday brunch. A cozy bistro tucked in a quiet Nob Hill neighborhood featuring delicious northern Italian cuisine. Loved by locals for great wine, ambience, and the ethereal tiramisu. No reservations, so get there early.

EMBARCADERO/FINANCIAL DISTRICT

Kokkari $$$ *200 Jackson Street, tel: 415-981-0983.* Open weekdays for lunch; dinner Monday through Saturday. An Aristotle Onassis sort of Greek taverna, with beamed ceilings, a massive fireplace, oriental carpets, and huge dishes of rich food. (Don't expect to see anyone intentionally smash a plate.) The crowd exudes a robust sense of well-being. Reservations are advised.

Plouf $$ *40 Belden Place, tel: 415-986-6491.* Open for lunch and dinner Monday through Friday; dinner only on Saturday. There are a number of good cafés with outdoor seating on Belden Place, a charming, brick alley off Bush and Kearny streets near the Financial District. Plouf specializes in delicious seafood prepared with a French accent, and the waiters also give the impression you've arrived in the Paris of the West.

Tadich Grill $$$ *240 California Street, tel: 415-391-1849.* Open for lunch and dinner Monday through Saturday. Tadich is a venerable institution that has been around in various incarnations since the gold rush, with wooden booths, white linen, and waiters as crusty as the sourdough. The menu of classics includes lobster Newburg and their signature cioppino. The cognoscenti order whatever fresh fish is available, grilled. Sidle up to the original mahogany bar, order a gin fizz, and soak in old-school San Francisco ambience.

SOMA

Thirsty Bear Brewing Company $$ *661 Howard Street, tel: 415-974-0905.* Open for lunch Monday through Saturday; dinner nightly. Excellent house-made beers and tasty Spanish tapas have made this spot a favorite. A nice selection of cheeses is offered with house made rye bread and macrona almonds but for more hearty fare try the paellas, *empanadas*, or bocadillos.

NORTH BEACH

Firenze by Night $$–$$$ *1429 Stockton Street, tel: 415-392-8485.* Open seven days a week for dinner. A traditional northern Italian restaurant in North Beach, right on the edge of Chinatown. It is deservedly famous for the outstanding pillowy-soft gnocchi, tender calamari and the pappardelle pasta Toscana with rabbit. Treat yourself to a glass of home-made *limoncello* with dessert.

L'Osteria del Forno $–$$ *519 Columbus Avenue, tel: 415-982-1124.* Open for lunch and dinner Wednesday through Monday. For casual but satisfying Italian food, including marvelous antipasti, thin-crusted pizzas, a daily pasta dish, and a fine roast pork loin braised in milk and herbs, and stellar focaccia sandwiches. This tiny treasure is a kid-pleaser as well. Cash only.

Tony's Pizza Napoletana $$ *1570 Stockton Street, tel: 415-835-9888.* Open for lunch and dinner Wednesday through Sunday. Nine-time World Pizza Champion Tony Gemignani fires up every imaginable style of pizza (East Coast, California, Chicago deep-dish, and of course Neapolitan) in wood-and coal-fired ovens at this family-friendly spot. A full menu of Italian dinners and appetizers is also available. Get there early, they don't take reservations.

CIVIC CENTER/HAYES VALLEY

Hayes Street Grill $$$ *320 Hayes Street, tel: 415-863-5545.* Open for lunch weekdays, dinner nightly. A local culinary institution, this restaurant features fresh sustainably caught seafood prepared simply, with integrity. Non-fish items include a juicy hamburger, housemade sausages, a Niman flank streak and organic salads. Local politicians eat lunch here; the pre-symphony, opera, and ballet crowd fill the tables before 8pm.

Zuni Café $$$ *1658 Market Street (Civic Center), tel: 415-552-2522.* Open for lunch Tuesday through Saturday, dinner Tuesday through Sunday, Sunday brunch. Make reservations and elbow your way past the crowded copper bar for the best roasted chicken with warm bread salad imaginable and other specialties from the wood-fired brick oven. The burger with shoestring potatoes has a cult following at this classic spot that has spawned legions of imitators. Actually, everything on the California-cuisine-based menu is great.

CASTRO

Chow $–$$ *215 Church Street, tel: 415-552-2469.* Open Monday through Saturday for breakfast, lunch, and dinner and Sunday brunch. For casual but well-prepared meals that will appeal to children and grown-ups, make your way to this popular place or its equally busy location on 9th Avenue by Golden Gate Park. Terrific pizzas, salads, sandwiches, brick-oven roasted chicken, and daily specials at prices that will amaze.

JAPANTOWN

Mifune $ *1737 Post Street, tel: 415-922-0337.* Lunch and dinner daily. The San Francisco branch of a famous Osaka restaurant proposes Japanese ramen, *udon* and *soba* in all their forms, often in steaming soups. This is the place for a quick lunch or dinner, and kids are very happy in the midst of all these noodles.

MARINA

A 16 $$–$$$ *2355 Chestnut Street, tel: 415-771-2216.* Open for lunch Wednesday through Friday, nightly for dinner. Southern Italy is the muse at this popular eatery that takes its name from the highway that runs from Naples to Puglia. Indulge in fresh pasta, house-cured meats, and authentic Neapolitan-style pizza and rub elbows with foodies in the know.

Greens $$–$$$ *Building A, Fort Mason, tel: 415-771-6222.* Open for lunch Tuesday through Saturday, dinner Monday through Saturday, and Sunday brunch. In a converted military warehouse on the bay, an airy upmarket vegetarian restaurant that even carnivores rave about. The Saturday evening *prix fixe* is a relative bargain and comes with lovely bay views. Reservations are essential.

THE MISSION DISTRICT

Delfina $$–$$$ *3621 18th Street, tel: 415-552-4055.* Open nightly for dinner. The kitchen in this noisy storefront restaurant turns out delicious Tuscan Italian food that provides a star turn for local, seasonal produce, fish, and meat. (If sea bass happens to be on the menu, catch it.) Reservations are essential, as this is a favorite neighborhood pick among residents from all over the city. If you can't get a table here, try their second location at 2406 California Street in Pacific Heights.

OUTSIDE THE CITY

OAKLAND

Bay Wolf Café $$–$$$ *3853 Piedmont Avenue, Oakland, tel: 510-655-6004.* Open for dinner nightly. This pioneer of California-style nouvelle cuisine has aged gracefully with sophistication serving rustic grilled Mediterranean-inspired specialties. The restaurant features a keenly chosen wine list with a nod to small production wineries.

Yoshi's $$ *510 Embarcadero West, Jack London Square, Oakland, tel: 510-238-9200.* Open for dinner nightly. The restaurant and lounge is adjacent to a world-class jazz club and serves good, if predictable, Japanese food and has a lively sushi bar. Diners receive priority seating in the legendary jazz club.

BERKELEY

Chez Panisse $$–$$$ *1517 Shattuck Avenue, Berkeley, tel: 510-548-5525, 510-548-5049 (café).* Open Monday through Saturday for dinner; the café is also open for lunch. Alice Waters's legendary restaurant is located in a redwood cottage and is the shrine for spectacularly tasty and original California cuisine. A *prix fixe* dinner is served at two seatings nightly. The upstairs café, which does not require reservations, is less expensive than the downstairs dining room, for which reservations are essential.

MARIN COUNTY

Guaymas $$–$$$ *5 Main Street, Tiburon, tel: 415-435-6300.* Open daily for lunch and dinner. Modern Mexican decor and cuisine combines with panoramas of San Francisco. A major hang-out for tourists and locals.

The Tavern at Lark Creek $$$ *234 Magnolia Avenue, Larkspur, tel: 415-924-7766.* Open for dinner nightly, Sunday brunch. Set among a few redwoods in the pretty town of Larkspur, you'll be treated to seasonal farm-to-table cuisine in a casual, homey ambiance. Great children's menu. Reservations required.

WINE COUNTRY

Bistro Jeanty $$ *6510 Washington Street, Yountville, tel: 707-944-0103.* Open for lunch and dinner daily. A very French bistro with an outdoor patio and spirited inside dining room and bar. The seasonal menu of homey dishes (including coq au vin, rabbit and sweetbread ragout, cassoulet, or a simple steak frites) is so satisfying you will want to eat here again and again.

The French Laundry $$$ *6640 Washington Street, Yountville, tel: 707-944-2380.* Open for lunch Friday through Sunday, dinner nightly. Plan ahead and save your money for this ultimate gastronomic splurge. At Chef Thomas Keller's world-renowned Napa Valley restaurant, obsessive detail, expert culinary technique, and inspired imagination conspire to create perfection on the plate. Go for it, if you can get in.

Tra Vigne $$$ *1050 Charter Oak Avenue, St Helena, tel: 707-963-4444.* Open daily for lunch and dinner, Sunday brunch. A large airy dining room opens onto a trellised patio with formidable stone tables and a whimsical fountain. The Italian fare is based on what's currently in the markets, and if it's tomato season, don't miss the fruits paired with fresh mozzarella. Reservations advised.

A–Z TRAVEL TIPS

A Summary of Practical Information

A

ACCOMMODATIONS (see also CAMPING, YOUTH HOSTELS, and the list of Recommended Hotels on page 133)

Some of the world's finest and most famous hotels contribute to San Francisco's reputation for hospitality. The more lavish among them offer sumptuous amenities that set them apart from the competition like expensive Italian-made sheets or bathrooms stocked with premium spa products. It is a good idea to make reservations well ahead of time especially if you plan to visit the during peak season from May to September. During winter, room rates tend to drop. For help booking rooms, call SF Reservations, tel: 800-677-1500 toll-free in US or 510-628-4400, or visit www.hotelres.com or www.sanfrancisco.travel. If you want to save on accommodations, consider one of the many motels on Lombard Street in the Marina. There are also a few youth hostels in the city that are low budget (www.sfhostels.com). On the web, www.bayarea.citysearch.com is a good resource for listings. Another option is to rent homes or apartments, an increasingly popular way to enjoy an authentic experience. For more information and listings, check out Vacation Rentals by Owner (www.vrbo.com).

All hotel rates in San Francisco are subject to a 14 percent room tax. Parking downtown can add another $20–25 per day, and telephone and Internet surcharges will also inflate the bill.

For a free Lodging Guide published annually by the San Francisco Convention and Visitors Bureau, tel: 415-391-9974 (toll-free in the US), visit www.onlyinsanfrancisco.com, or write to them at 900 Market Street, San Francisco, CA 94103-2804.

AIRPORTS

San Francisco International Airport (SFO; tel: 800-435-9736; www.flysfo.com) is one of the busiest airports in the US, handling international connections for the Pacific Rim, Europe, and Latin America. Facilities at SFO are excellent, particularly in the International Terminal. The airport is on the freeway 14 miles (23km) south of the city – half an hour by taxi but a bit longer during the rush hour. A BART station has been added for easy transport to the city center. Be advised that BART runs from approximately 4am to 11.45pm. Information booths, with multilingual staff, are located near baggage-claim areas in each terminal.

Taxis are always available outside the doors of the arrival area. The fare to downtown is around $50 plus tip. Shuttle vans are available at center islands outside the upper-level departure terminals. They provide door-to-door service for approximately $17 (before tip) per person; advance reservations are not necessary. If you plan to rent a car, a courtesy bus or the BART rapid transit line *(see page 129)* will deposit you at the rental car building.

An alternative to SFO Airport is the less hectic Oakland International Airport across the Bay. A shuttle bus links the airport to the BART rapid-transit line to downtown San Francisco. Otherwise, taxis and shuttle buses are available outside the airline terminals.

B

BICYCLE RENTAL

There are miles of agreeable cycling routes in throughout the city and Golden Gate Park, and on Sundays John F. Kennedy Drive is closed to automobile traffic, so you can cycle nearly to the beach free of exhaust fumes. Bikes may be rented on Stanyan Street near the park's eastern boundary for around $30–50 per day (depending on the type of bike). Cycling across the Golden Gate Bridge is also enjoyable (if windy), and at least two rental companies (Bay City Bike in Fisherman's Wharf; tel: 415-346-2453; www.baycitybike.com; and Blazing Saddles; tel: 415-202-8888; www.blazingsaddles.com) offer a bike tour to Sausalito with a return trip by ferry. Cycling is a popular way of exploring the wine country north of San Francisco, with rentals and tours available in Sonoma, St Helena, and Calistoga.

BUDGETING FOR YOUR TRIP

San Francisco isn't an inexpensive destination. The average daily expenditure per visitor is approximately $332 according to the Convention and Visitors Bureau, with the bulk of expenses divided between lodging and food. While many hotels offer weekend and off-season rates, there isn't a true low season in the city.

Accommodations. Plan to pay from $125 for a modest motel room outside Union Square to $185 on up for a small but smartly decorated room at the city's finer boutique hotels.

Meals. The price for a three-course dinner in a mid-range restaurant is approximately $35. You can easily spend under $15 per person for a great Chinese, Mexican, Salvadoran, Vietnamese, Thai, or Japanese meal (among others) by exploring the respective neighborhoods. Typically a beer will cost around $4 to $6 at bars and restaurants with wine and cocktails being a bit more. Many bars offer Happy Hour from about 5 to 7pm.

Transportation. Buses and Muni cost $2 and you'll receive a transfer good for a second trip within two hours. Cab fare runs $2.85 for the base fee and $2.25 per additional mile. Parking fees are hefty downtown and at Fisherman's Wharf, where the garage at Pier 39 charges $7 per hour.

Attractions. Some of the best attractions in town are free, including the Golden Gate Bridge, Chinatown, and Golden Gate Park. Museum admissions begin at $18 for adults (half for kids) at the major museums though they offer monthly free days and discounted evenings, and a daytime tour to Alcatraz will set a couple back over $60.

C

CAMPING

There are campsites in state parks outside San Francisco in Marin County and Half Moon Bay, but camping is not allowed in the city. For information, write to California Department of Parks and

Recreation, Attention Publications Office, PO Box 942896, Sacramento, CA 94296. National Parks Service information is available from Building 201, Fort Mason, San Francisco, CA 94123.

CAR RENTAL/HIRE

Driving and parking in the city can be an unpleasant experience at best, and if you can avoid renting a car, do so. For trips outside the city, rent from one of the many firms located around Union Square. At the airport and downtown, every national firm is represented (Avis, Budget, Hertz, National, and Enterprise). It's worth shopping around. rices vary widely under the laws of supply and demand, according to the season, and even within a single firm on the same day. Look into special weekly and weekend rates and Internet specials, but budget at least $50 per day, not including parking fees.

Automatic transmission and air-conditioning are standard. Note that rates which sound reasonable can end up much higher when insurance is added. Check your auto insurance policy to see if you are fully covered for rentals before accepting the 'collision damage waiver' option. Renters need a valid driver's license plus an International Driving Permit if you reside outside the US or Canada. Most agencies set a minimum age for car rental at 25, some at 21, and a credit card is required.

CLIMATE

The biggest surprise for visitors is that summer can be very chilly. Those people shivering in shorts are uninformed tourists. If they had driven an hour inland they might be sweltering in tropical sunshine, but the famous fog that often shrouds the city (particularly in summer) keeps the temperature down. Oddly, the warmest season is autumn. Of course, it doesn't take much to constitute a heatwave in San Francisco. Winters are cold, often rainy, and sometimes windy.

To help you with predictions, over the page are the average daily maximum and minimum temperatures by month for San Francisco.

	J	F	M	A	M	J	J	A	S	O	N	D
°C	13	15	16	17	17	19	18	18	21	20	17	14
°F	55	59	61	62	63	66	65	65	69	68	63	57
°C	7	8	9	9	11	11	12	12	13	12	11	8
°F	45	47	48	49	51	52	53	53	55	54	51	47

CLOTHING

The mornings are often quite chilly, warming significantly by mid-afternoon, then plunging down again in the evening. Wearing layers like the locals do is the best way to feel comfortable: you can adapt to the changing temperatures by removing or adding a piece of clothing. A sweater or jacket is likely to be welcome for at least part of every day; an all-weather coat will come in handy in winter. Comfortable walking shoes go a long way toward taming the hills.

San Franciscans have succumbed to an informal dress code and casual clothes are acceptable nearly everywhere you go.

CRIME AND SAFETY

With a relatively low crime rate for a large city, San Francisco poses no special dangers. Take cabs late at night, don't walk unescorted in the small hours, and avoid the mysteries of dark streets or run-down areas. There is obvious homelessness and drug trade in the Tenderloin, Civic Center, and some blocks of mid-Market/SoMa. Leave valuables in your hotel safe, and beware of pickpockets in crowded places and on Muni. The all-purpose emergency telephone number is **911.** For less urgent police business, tel: 415-553-0123.

D

DISABLED TRAVELERS

Contact the San Francisco Convention and Visitors Bureau for a guide offering detailed access information on more than 100 San Francisco-area hotels, restaurants and attractions, as well as information on accessible transportation, local organizations for individuals with disabilities, wheelchair rentals, and medical supply dealers.

A free *Access San Francisco* visitor kit can be ordered from the SFCVB online at www.sanfrancisco.travel, by email at vic1@sanfrancisco.travel, or by calling 415-391-2000 or 415-392-0328 TTY. Copies are also available at the SFCVB Visitor Information Center located on the lower level of Hallidie Plaza, 900 Market Street.

DRIVING

The United States is the land of the car, but when it comes to San Francisco, it's best not to drive, except for out-of-town trips. The hills and parking problems exacerbate the normal hazards of city driving.

The regulations are straightforward. Drive on the right, pass on the left. Unless there's a sign to the contrary, you can turn right on a red signal, providing that you stop and check that no pedestrians or traffic deter this maneuver. Drivers and all passengers must wear seatbelts; children under six years require carseats or booster seats. Cable cars always have the right of way, as do pedestrians at the designated crosswalks. School buses (painted yellow) are given special priority by law; it is a serious offense to pass a school bus *in either direction* on a two-lane road when it is taking on or discharging passengers.

Highways. California has no toll roads, though you have to pay to cross the Golden Gate Bridge or the San Francisco-Oakland Bay Bridge. (Fares are collected only as you arrive in San Francisco.) The freeway system is complicated enough to deserve advanced planning; if you miss an exit you can lose a lot of time trying to double back.

Speed limits. On Interstate highways the limit is normally 65mph (105km/h). On all other highways the limit is 55mph (90km/h).

Parking. 'Curbing' the wheels of a parked car is the law in San Francisco, so that if a car rolls downhill the curb will brake it. Parking downhill, turn your wheels toward the curb; parking uphill, away from the curb. Engage the handbrake and put the car in gear. Parking meters govern the time you can stay in some areas and some only accept coins. Elsewhere in the city a color code indicates the restrictions. A red curb means no parking at all, green represents a ten-minute parking limit, yellow is a loading zone, and white is a no-parking zone permitting passenger loading only. The tow-trucks mean business, especially if you block a fire hydrant or a bus stop. Read the posted signs on all streets for street-cleaning days and other parking restrictions, including no parking rules on downtown streets between 3 and 6pm.

Fuel. Most gas (petrol) stations are self-service and are equipped to accept credit cards for payment at the pump. 'Full-serve' is more expensive, but it may include a window-cleaning. Gas stations are open every day from early in the morning until 10pm or later.

Breakdowns and services. The American Automobile Association (AAA; www.aaa.com) offers assistance to members of affiliated organizations abroad. In San Francisco the AAA-affiliated automobile club is the California State Automobile Association, 599 Clement Street; tel: 415-750-7800. In case of breakdown, dial 800-AAA-Help (toll-free) for information on how to obtain emergency assistance.

E

EARTHQUAKES

Basically, the Bay Area is in the line of fire. If you feel a tremor while you're indoors, stay there, preferably beneath a sturdy piece of furniture like a desk or table. Outdoors, avoid trees, power lines, and the walls of buildings. In a car, sit it out by the side of the road, but away from power lines and bridges. If you want to be prepared for the worst, study the San Francisco telephone directory, which contains four pages of earthquake instructions. If you'd like to find out what a tremor feels like, stop by the California Academy of Sciences and check out the earthquake exhibit.

ELECTRICITY

Throughout the United States the standard is 110 volts, 60-cycle AC Plugs have two flat prongs. Overseas visitors without dual-voltage travel appliances will need a transformer and adapter plug for appliances such as an electric razor or a hairdryer.

EMBASSIES AND CONSULATES

All embassies in the US are in Washington, DC, but some countries also maintain consulates in San Francisco. To find the address of a consulate, look in the alphabetical listings of the telephone directory under 'Consulates' or in the *Yellow Pages* under 'Consulates and Other Foreign Government Representatives.'
Australia: 575 Market Street, Suite, tel: 415-644-3620.
Canada: 550 South Hope Street, 9th Floor, Los Angeles, tel: 213-346-2700.
Ireland: 100 Pine Street, Suite 3350, tel: 415-392-4214.
New Zealand: 1200 Wilshire Boulevard, Los Angeles, CA, tel: 415-399-1255.
South Africa: 6300 Wilshire Boulevard, Suite 600, Los Angeles 90048, tel: 323-651-0902.
United Kingdom: 1 Sansome Street, Suite 850, tel: 415-617-1300.

EMERGENCIES (see also HEALTH AND MEDICAL CARE and POLICE)

The all-purpose number to call in any emergency is **911**. You can call from any telephone; no coins are required. The operator will note the information and relay it to the police, ambulance, or the fire department, accordingly.

G

GAY AND LESBIAN TRAVELERS

San Francisco is, arguably, the 'gayest' city in the US. Most of the scene is concentrated in the Castro and SoMa neighborhoods, but you will find gay establishments in other areas as well. The *Bay Area Reporter* has the most comprehensive listings and is available free. Most of the lesbian community is centered around Valencia Street and Noe Valley. San Francisco is very tolerant of alternative lifestyles and considered a safe haven for the gay community.

Resources for gay, lesbian and transgender travelers include www.onlyinsanfrancisco.com/gaytravel and www.advocate.com/travel.asp.

GETTING THERE

By air. Dozens of international flights serve San Francisco daily. The major carriers offer non-stop flights from Europe to San Francisco, or connections via New York, Chicago, or Los Angeles. There are non-stop or one-stop flights from the principal Pacific airports. Beyond the standard first-class, business/club, and economy fares, the principal cost-cutting possibilities are variations of APEX (book 21 days before departure for stays of seven days to six months). Off-season reduced fares and package deals are also available. Certain US airlines offer bargains for foreign travelers who visit several American destinations.

From North America, direct flights connect American and Canadian cities to San Francisco. Special fares are available on these highly competitive routes, and prices frequently change. Fly-drive vacations are offered by many airlines. Consult travel websites www.travelocity.com, www.expedia.com, www.orbitz.com, www.uptake.com, www.hotwire.com, or other travel discounters on the Internet.

Airports in the nearby cities of Oakland and San Jose are also options for travelers visiting San Francisco.

By rail. Amtrak, the passenger railway company, goes only as far as Oakland, where special shuttle buses take passengers to the Ferry Building at Market and Embarcadero streets in San Francisco. The *California Zephyr* links Oakland with Chicago and Denver. The *Coast Starlight* stops in Oakland on the way from Portland and Seattle to Los Angeles and San Diego. In the US, telephone 800-USA-RAIL (toll-free); www.amtrak.com.

By bus. Long-distance Greyhound buses use the Transbay Terminal. For more information about bus services across the continent, telephone Greyhound toll-free at 800-231-2222; www.greyhound.com.
By car. The excellent Interstate freeway system criss-crosses all of the United States. Odd numbers designate freeways running north to south, while even-numbered Interstates run east to west. Interstate 101, for instance, serves the length of California, entering San Francisco via the Golden Gate Bridge and leaving near the airport.

GUIDES AND TOURS

San Francisco tour companies offer bus, boat, bike, and walking excursions aimed at the broadest or narrowest interest, from a one-hour glimpse of the city's highlights aboard a simulated cable car to a walking (and eating and shopping) tour of Chinatown or the Castro. Leaflets listing the possibilities proliferate in hotel lobbies and the Visitor Information Center at Powell and Market streets. Bargain-hunters and anyone interested in the history and architecture of San Francisco should contact City Guides (tel: 415-557-4266; www.sfcityguides.org). They run approximately 30 different free tours each month on a wide variety of interesting topics and in different parts of the city. Maps for the stunning 49-mile (79km) Scenic Drive tour can be picked up at the Convention and Visitors Bureau's Visitor Information Center. This is a self-guided driving tour of San Francisco. It takes approximately four to five hours to drive, depending on how often you stop.

Tours of Alcatraz are excellent and very popular, there is even a spooky night tour (tel: 888-814-2305; www.alcatraztickets.com). Some good walking tours include Cruisin' the Castro (tel: 415-255-1821; www.cruisinthecastro.com) that centers on gay life in San Francisco; GraceAnn Walden's food lovers tours of North Beach, Chinatown, and the Mission (tel: 415-302-5898; www.graceann walden.net/tours), and FOOT Comedy Walking Tours (tel: 415-793-5378; www.foottours.com).

H

HEALTH AND MEDICAL CARE

Everywhere in the United States health care is private and extremely expensive, especially hospitalization, which can quickly become an economic disaster. It is essential, before you leave home, to sign up for medical insurance covering your stay. This can be arranged through an insurance company or agent or through your travel agent as part of a travel insurance package.

Tap water is perfectly safe to drink everywhere in the Bay Area.

Drugstores (pharmacies). Many drugstores of the Walgreens chain stay open 24 hours a day; in others, pharmacists are available until midnight. Check the store locator at www.walgreens.com or with your hotel to find out where the nearest one is. You may find that some medicines obtainable over the counter in your home country are available only by prescription in the US, and vice versa.

L

LIQUOR LAWS

Liquor is sold in supermarkets and even some drugstores, but not between 2am and 6am. The same schedule restrictions affect restaurants and bars; some can serve only beer and wine. You may be asked to prove you are over 21, the legal age for drinking in California.

M

MAPS

Maps of San Francisco are sold at bookstores, news kiosks, and gas stations. A comprehensive map of the city's streets and public transport system is sold by Muni, the San Francisco Municipal Railway. Free tourist magazines usually include maps of the most popular areas as well as at the Visitor's Center at Powell and Market (downstairs).

MEDIA

The major daily newspaper in town is the *San Francisco Chronicle*. Delivered in the morning, it is available from sidewalk kiosks and often at your hotel's front desk. On Sunday, the *Chronicle* publishes a larger edition which includes the 'pink section,' a comprehensive guide to arts and culture listings and reviews. On Thursdays, a section called '96 Hours' is devoted to the same type of information for the weekend ahead. The *Chronicle*'s website, www.sfgate.com, is widely visited and contains a wealth of information about the city as well as providing up-to-the-minute news coverage.

Kiosks, newsstands, and racks around town offer plenty of other choices for news both national and local. Two local tabloids that are published weekly are the *Bay Guardian* and *SF Weekly*; both are great sources for up-to-date listings and information about upcoming events in the city.

Almost every hotel room has radio and television with a vast selection of channels, including programmes in a wide range of foreign languages. The nationwide commercial networks are found on channels 2, 4, 5, and 7, and channel 9 is the local affiliate of Public Broadcasting Service (PBS), which, as a rule, has a higher-quality output and is commercial-free. Most hotels also have cable TV.

On the radio, dial 810AM for news, weather and traffic reports.

MONEY

Currency. The dollar ($) is divided into 100 cents (¢).

Banknotes: $1, $5, $10, $20, $50, and $100. Larger denominations are not in general circulation. All notes are the same size and the same black-and-green color, so be sure to double-check your cash before you dispense it.

Coins: 1¢ (penny), 5¢ (nickel), 10¢ (dime), 25¢ (quarter), 50¢ (half dollar), and $1.

Banks and currency exchange. Banks are open from 9am to 5pm, Monday to Thursday, until 6pm Friday, and some operate on Saturday morning as well. You can change foreign currency at the airport, at leading banks downtown, and at bureaux de change in areas frequented by tourists or financiers. ATMs have become the most popular way to get cash; they are accessible any time of day and are found on the street, inside some stores, in lobbies of buildings and outside banks.

Credit cards. When buying something or paying a restaurant bill you may be asked, 'Cash or charge?' Most Americans carry a variety of credit cards, and they are accepted in most places.

Traveler's checks. It is wise to buy traveler's checks denominated in US$. Foreign currency traveler's checks must be exchanged at a bank.

Sales taxes. In the absence of VAT, cities and states around the US levy sales taxes and other hidden extras. An 8½ percent sales tax is added to the price of all goods and services in San Francisco.

O

OPENING HOURS

Shops. Hours tend to vary from shop to shop and district to district, but most department stores operate daily from 10am to 8.30 or 9pm, Saturday. Note that a number of smaller shops close on Sunday.

Museums. Hours vary, but 10am–5pm is your best bet; most are closed one weekday.

Banks. Hours are generally Mon–Fri 9am–5pm , though some stay open longer.

Post offices. Branches stay open from 8.30 or 9am to 5 or 5.30pm Mon–Fri.

P

POLICE

The blue-uniformed city police, some of them multilingual, are courteous and helpful to tourists. Imitating a feature of Japanese life, they operate *kobans* or mini police stations at Market and Powell streets; in Chinatown on Grant Avenue between Washington and Jackson streets; and in Japantown at Post and Buchanan streets. Out of town on roads, you'll encounter the California Highway Patrol in tan uniforms with ranger hats. In an emergency dial **911**. For non-emergency situations, call 415-553-0123. Central Station is located in North Beach, close to Chinatown at 622 Vallejo Street, tel: 415-315-2400.

POST OFFICES

The US postal service deals only with mail. A branch post office in the basement of Macy's department store, Union Square, is convenient. A large post office is located downtown at 101 Market Street, at Spear Street near The Embarcadero. Most neighborhoods have their own branches; check the branch locator at www.usps.com or the *Yellow Pages* for the exact location. Dark blue post office boxes that are labelled and contain the US Postal logo are scattered around the city and post offices fly American flags, making it easier to identify them. Many ATMs also sell stamps.

PUBLIC HOLIDAYS

Banks, post offices, government buildings, and some businesses are closed on the following major holidays:

January 1	New Year's Day
Third Monday in January	Martin Luther King Day
Third Monday in February	Presidents' Day
Last Monday in May	Memorial Day
July 4	Independence Day
First Monday in September	Labor Day
Second Monday in October	Columbus Day
November 11	Veterans' Day
Last Thursday in November	Thanksgiving
December 25	Christmas Day

R

RELIGION

Every religious denomination has a house of worship in San Francisco. The Saturday newspapers list times of some of the services. The Visitor Information Center *(see page 128)* has a list of church addresses. While formal attire is not usually necessary at most places of worship, dressing respectfully is a good general rule. For a rousing, gospel music-filled Sunday service, show up a half-hour before the 9am or 11am celebration at Glide Memorial Church, 330 Ellis Street (tel: 415-674-6000).

S

SMOKING

Smoking is prohibited in public places such as office buildings, schools, libraries, public restrooms, and service or check-out lines. In liberal San Francisco, it's even banned in bars and restaurants. Some buildings have designated smoking areas outside in front.

T

TELEPHONES

The American telephone system is run by private, regional companies. Coin- or card-operated phones are found in all public places – hotel lobbies, drugstores, gas stations, bars, restaurants, and along the streets. Directions for use are clearly stated on the machine. For local directory assistance dial 411 or 555-1212 (free of charge). When calling long-distance, the rules of competition mean that you often have to choose between companies by pushing one or another button; to the visitor it scarcely matters which. Evening (after 6pm) and weekend rates are much cheaper. Many hotels, airlines, and business firms have toll-free numbers (beginning 800, 888, or 877) so you can avoid long-distance charges. In hotels, you might need need to dial 9 to get a dial tone before the phone number and 1 before the area code.

In order to use a US SIM card you need to ensure your phone is unlocked and quad band. If so, you can purchase a card from any mobile phone store (which are numerous: AT&T, T-Mobile). However, this will not be a cheap option for international calls you may want to use pre-paid phone cards to call from a land line instead.

Some hotels add a hefty surcharge to their guests' outgoing calls, local or long-distance.

The area code for the city of San Francisco is 415. The area code for most of the East Bay area, including Oakland and Berkeley, is 510, and 650 is the area code for the peninsula (south of San Francisco).

TIME ZONES

The continental United States is divided into four time zones. San Francisco is in the Pacific zone, which is eight hours behind GMT. Between the first Sunday in April and the last Sunday in October, the clock is advanced one hour for Daylight Saving Time (GMT minus seven hours). The following chart shows the time in various cities when it is noon in San Francisco.

San Francisco	Chicago	New York	London	Paris
noon	2pm	3pm	8pm	9pm

TIPPING

Service is never included in restaurant prices, but it is sometimes added to the bill. In restaurants and bars, tip 15–20 percent of the total bill; even in informal coffee shops, tips are expected as a general rule of business. In general, porters are tipped $1–2 per bag; maids $1–2 per day; cloakroom attendants and doormen who find you a taxi, $1; taxi drivers and hairdressers, 15–20 percent.

TOILETS

Some dark-green coin-operated public bathrooms are located near tourist sites on Market Street and Fisherman's Wharf. Many restaurants discourage anyone but patrons from using their facilities; your best bet is to try a department store, hotel, gas station, or fast-food chain restaurant.

TOURIST INFORMATION

For advance inquiries, write to the San Francisco Convention & Visitors Bureau, 201 Third Street, Suite 900, San Francisco, CA 94103. The bureau offers a variety of information kits available on their website; most packages are free. You could also contact the US Embassy, Visit USA Committee, or USTTA (United States Travel and Tourism Administration) in your own country:

Australia: Suite 6106, MLC Center, King and Castlereagh Streets, Sydney, New South Wales 2000.
Canada: 800 Rochester Boulevard, West Suite 1110, Montreal, Quebec H3B 1X9.
Ireland: Irish Visit USA Committee, c/o Tour America, 62 Middle Abbey Street, Dublin; tel: (353) (1) 662-0860.
New Zealand: Visit USA Commitee, 129A Kohimarama Road, Kohimarama, Auckland; tel: (64) (9) 528 4447.
South Africa: US Embassy, PO Box 9536, Pretoria 0001; tel: (271) (2) 342-1048.
UK: 22 Sackville Street, London W1X 2EA; tel: (020) 7439 7433.

In San Francisco: San Francisco's Visitor Information Center www.sfvisitor.org or www.onlyinsanfrancisco.com is located on the lower level of Hallidie Plaza at Market and Powell streets, near the cable-car terminus. The office is open Mon–Fri 9am–5pm, Sat–Sun 9am–3pm, closed on Sun from Nov–Apr and on major holidays. Telephone inquiries: 415-391-2000. A recorded message listing daily events is available on tel: 415-391-2001. (For Italian, tel: 415-391-2002; German, tel: 415-391-2004; Spanish, tel: 415-391-2122; Japanese, tel: 415-391-2101.)

TRANSPORTATION

Muni Metro lines operate underground in the downtown district, above ground beyond. There are five lines, making the same Market Street stops as the BART system. Muni buses and historic streetcars zigzag above ground to all parts of the city. Board buses through the front door and leave from the rear. The exact fare is required; drivers don't give change. A two-part transfer slip is provided when you pay your fare on buses, streetcars, and Metro lines. This transfer allows you to transfer two more times to any bus, streetcar or Metro line within a 90-minute time-frame. No transfers are given or accepted on cable cars; single fares must be paid each time you board. The problem of needing exact change is avoided if you buy a Muni pass valid for a full day (or three days or a week) on all lines, including the cable cars. Three- and seven-day Visitor Passports allow unlimited rides. The passes are on sale at the Visitor Information Center *(see page 128)* and other locations.

Cable cars, on three lines, go over the hills to the principal areas of tourist interest. Tickets are sold on board, and drivers will make change. The cable cars are usually crowded, mostly with tourists enjoying the invigorating ride. Never board or leave a cable car until it has stopped; get off facing the direction of travel.

BART, the pioneering Bay Area Rapid Transit system, offers a fast, quiet, comfortable rail service between San Francisco and stations in the East and South Bay areas as well as to the Oakland and San Francisco International Airports. To get to the Oakland airport you must board a shuttle from BART. Maps and charts in the stations explain the routes and the computerized ticketing system. There are change-giving machines alongside the coin-operated ticket-dispensing machines.

Intercity buses operate from the Transbay Terminal, at First and Mission streets. AC Transit crosses the Bay Bridge to Berkeley, Oakland, and other East Bay communities. Golden Gate Transit uses the Golden Gate Bridge to serve Marin and Sonoma counties. Samtrans is the San Mateo County service, going as far as Palo Alto.

Taxis are usually plentiful in touristy areas. They congregate at the luxury hotels, but you can hail one in the street. If you're staying in an out-of-the-way location, it's convenient to telephone for a radio-dispatched taxi.

Ferryboats seemed to be doomed when the bridges were built, but they still provide a useful service for commuters and tourists. The principal terminals are the Ferry Building, at the foot of Market Street, and Piers 39 to 41/2. The Blue and Gold Fleet, which does big business in Bay sightseeing cruises, also goes to Oakland, Alameda, and Alcatraz. Golden Gate Ferries go to Sausalito and Larkspur. The Red and White Fleet cruises to Sausalito, Tiburon, and Vallejo.

V

VISAS AND ENTRY REQUIREMENTS

Canadians traveling by air must present a valid passport for entry. Visitors from the UK, Australia, New Zealand, and Ireland qualify for the visa waiver program, and therefore do not need a visa for stays of less than 90 days, as long as they have a valid ten-year machine-readable passport and a return ticket. However, they must apply online for authorization at least 72 hours before traveling at https://esta.cbp.dhs.gov. Citizens of South Africa need a visa. All foreign visitors have their two index fingers scanned and a digital photograph taken at the port of entry. The process takes only 10–15 seconds.

Red and green channels are in use at America's international airports, and all formalities are simpler and quicker than in the past. If you fly in, you should be given the customs and immigration forms to complete well before landing. Cigarettes, cigars, tobacco, wine and spirits have the usual limits. A non-resident may take into the US gifts, free of duty and taxes, to a value of $800. The import of plants, seeds, vegetables, fruits, or other fresh food is prohibited; foods of all kinds are subject to inspection. If you're carrying money and checks totaling more than $10,000 in or out of the country, they must be reported.

W

WEBSITES AND INTERNET CAFÉS

These web sites are full of information to help you get a head start on your vacation.

www.bayarea.citysearch.com A comprehensive, regularly updated site devoted to all things San Francisco, including arts, entertainment, dining, and attractions.

www.craigslist.org Event listings, house swaps, and other general information.

www.sfbg.com The *San Francisco Bay Guardian* site, with event listings and the low-down on nightlife.

www.sfgate.com The *San Francisco Chronicle* website.

www.sfweekly.com Catering to young urbanites, *SF Weekly*'s site has complete entertainment listings.

www.sfstation Entertainment, restaurant, arts, and events listings. Very thorough and cutting-edge.

www.sanfrancisco.travel The Convention and Visitors Bureau site is packed with tons of useful information for travelers.

www.yelp.com A site for real people to review all manner of restaurants, bars, shops, cafés, and services. Valuable insight can be gleaned here.

www.511.org Useful for information on all forms of Bay Area transportation.

www.wunderground.com/us/ca/san_francisco Detailed short- and long-range weather forecasts.

www.mistersf.com A quirky collection of San Francisco anecdotes, history, contemporary culture, and characters.

You can check your email and surf the Internet while traveling at the many cafés around the city that offer free Wi-Fi and at all public libraries. Branches of the ubiquitous Starbucks chain offer free Internet access.

WEIGHTS AND MEASURES

Efforts to ease the United States into the metric system are proceeding slowly. The government itself is said to be converting to international measurements, and indeed the national parks use kilometers, but in real life it's still inches, feet, yards, miles, and degrees Fahrenheit.

Y

YOUTH HOSTELS

The Golden Gate Council of American Youth Hostels operates budget accommodation at Union Square and Fort Mason, as well as hostels in scenic locations around the Bay area.

The address of the Union Square installation, with lodgings for 175 people, is 312 Mason Street, San Francisco, CA 94102; tel: 415-788-5604.

You can contact the Fort Mason Hostel, capacity 150, at Building 240, Fort Mason, San Francisco, CA 94123; tel: 415-771-7277.

In Sausalito, you can try the Golden Gate Youth Hostel, 941 Fort Barry, Sausalito, CA 94965; tel: 415-331-2777.

Additional hostels are listed in the Lodging Guide issued by the San Francisco Convention & Visitors Bureau *(see page 128)*.

Note that advance booking is essential at all Youth Hostels in San Francisco. For more information, contact: Hostelling International USA, 8401 Colesville Road, Suite 600, Silver Spring, MD 20910; tel: 301-495-1240; www.hiusa.org.

Recommended Hotels

San Francisco has a dizzying array of hotels, motels, bed and breakfasts, and inns, that range from dull to dramatic. Some of the more interesting rooms are located in small, boutique hotels, that often have unique flair and personality and offer perks like free Wi-fi access, complimentary wine receptions, and in-room coffee.

Whether a boutique, a B&B, or a 1,000-room behemoth that will honor your frequent-flier mileage, all the hotels listed below are clean and offer excellent service. Rooms will generally include cable television and direct-dial telephones, but not air-conditioning (it isn't really necessary). Be sure to ask about Internet and parking charges as many established hotel chains charge exorbitant fees for both.

Since San Francisco is a very popular convention and tourist town, it is a good idea to make reservations well ahead of time especially if you plan to visit the during peak season from May to September. During winter, room rates tend to drop. Bear in mind also that a hefty hotel tax of 14 percent is added to your final room total.

The prices below refer to high-season rack rates for a standard double room, exclusive of taxes (14 percent). Prices do not include parking or breakfast unless otherwise noted. When making reservations at the larger hotels, it is always worth inquiring about special packages and discounts.

$$$$$	over $250
$$$$	$200–250
$$$	$150–200
$$	$125–150
$	below $125

UNION SQUARE

Andrews Hotel $–$$ *624 Post Street, SF 94109, tel: 415-563-6877, tel: 800-926-3739 (toll-free in US), www.andrewshotel.com.* A 1905 Victorian well located two blocks west of Union Square. The rooms and baths are on the small side, but rates include a continental breakfast and evening wine reception.

Campton Place Hotel $$$$$ *340 Stockton Street, SF 94108, tel: 415-781-5555, www.tajhotels.com.* Elegant, luxurious, and intimate, this is one of the most renowned and refined hotels in the city. The service is excellent, the amenities are top-notch, and the hotel restaurant consistently merits the highest ratings. Wheelchair-accessible.

Chancellor Hotel $$–$$$ *433 Powell Street, SF 94102, tel: 415-362-2004*, tel: *800-428-4748 (toll-free in US), www.chancellorhotel.com.* The same family has owned and managed this charming hotel since 1917. It is situated on the Powell Street cable-car line and within a stone's throw of the major department stores around Union Square. Rooms are comfortably furnished in classic European style; baths are small but well stocked.

Hotel Frank $$$–$$$$ *386 Geary Street, SF 94102, tel: 415-986-2000, tel: 877-838-4478 (toll-free in US), www.hotelfranksf.com.* Hip and stylish, this boutique hotel is eco-friendly and offers free Wi-fi, iPod speaker docks, and two ultra-chic penthouse lofts. Max's on the Square, featuring delicious deli fare, is on the premises.

Galleria Park Hotel $$$–$$$$$ *191 Sutter Street, SF 94104, tel: 415-781-3060, tel: 800-792-9639 (toll-free in US), www.galleria park.com.* A boutique hotel with 17 suites convenient to both Union Square and the Financial District, with a comfortable, home-style feel. It's a favorite with business travelers. Complimentary Wi-Fi throughout the hotel, an evening wine reception, daily morning coffee and tea service, and complimentary newspapers.

Golden Gate Hotel $–$$$ *775 Bush Street, SF 94108, tel: 415-392-3702, tel: 800-835-1118 (toll-free in US), www.goldengatehotel.com.* A cozy family-run hotel near Union Square and two blocks from the Chinatown Gate. The pretty rooms contain few amenities, but the hotel's rates include a continental breakfast and afternoon tea with 'good, strong coffee and real English tea'. Smoking is not allowed in the hotel. Some rooms with private bath. Pet-friendly.

Grant Plaza Hotel $–$$ *465 Grant Avenue, SF 94108, tel: 415-434-3883, tel: 800-472-6899 (toll-free in US), www.grantplaza.*

com. Just one block up Grant Avenue from the Chinatown Gate, on the corner of Pine Street, this excellent-value hotel enjoys a superb location at the edge of Chinatown and a stone's throw from the Financial District and Union Square. The rooms are on the small side, but the staff are friendly and have plenty of local tips.

Handlery Union Square Hotel $$$ *351 Geary Street, SF 94102, tel: 415-781-7800, tel: 800-843-4343 (toll-free in US), www.handlery.com/sf.* A good choice for families, the hotel has a heated pool, morning and evening room service, even Nintendo games. Unique suites, located in an adjacent building, are large and offer dressing areas, robes, newspapers, and fresh decor. Wheelchair-accessible.

Hotel des Arts $–$$ *447 Bush Street, SF 94108, tel: 415-956-3232, tel: 800-956-0399 (toll-free in US), www.sfhoteldesarts.com.* This is the place for the thrifty art aficionado. Modest rooms are canvasses for edgy, emerging talent, each showcasing a different artistic vision. Despite the affordable price, there is free Wi-fi, Continental breakfast, refrigerators, and concierge service.

The Inn at Union Square $$$–$$$$$ *440 Post Street, SF 94102, tel: 415-397-3510, tel: 800-288-4346 (toll-free in US), www.unionsquare.com.* Some of the ways in which this hotel goes the extra distance include bottled spring water on the nightstand, early evening wine and hors d'oeuvres in front of the fireplace for guests and their associates, and an overnight shoe-shining service. The nearby full-service fitness club has a heated lap pool and well-equipped gym. Smoking is not allowed in the hotel. Wheelchair-accessible.

Kensington Park Hotel $$$–$$$$ *450 Post Street, SF 94102, tel: 415-788-6400, tel: 800-553-1900 (toll-free in US), www.kensingtonparkhotel.com.* Elegant rooms and baths distinguish this fine hotel, which is next door to Farallon, a highly regarded seafood restaurant where guests are assured preferred seating. Rates include afternoon tea and sherry; free Wi-Fi; concierge services are friendly and helpful. The hotel is also pet-friendly.

King George Hotel $$–$$$ *334 Mason Street, SF 94102, tel: 415-781-5050, tel: 800-288-6005 (toll-free in US), www.kinggeorge.com.* Opened in 1912, this British hotel champions old-fashioned rates and hospitality combined with up-to-date services. Winston's Bar and Lounge is open evenings and offers wine, champagne, and specialty beers. Complimentary in-room internet access.

Larkspur Hotel $$–$$$$ *524 Sutter Street, SF 94102, tel: 415-421-2865, tel: 800-919-9779 (toll-free in US), www.cartwrighthotel.com.* This genteel hotel has tastefully decorated rooms and plenty of amenities. Morning coffee and tea service is included and they offer access to a complimentary business center and free Wi-fi. Five suites are available, a plus for families. Pets are welcome.

Hotel Monaco $$$$ *501 Geary Street, SF 94102, tel: 415-292-0100, tel: 866-622-5284 (toll-free in US), www.hotelmonaco.com.* Rooms in this hotel are comfortable and glamorous, featuring lots of color and texture. Amenities include complimentary newspapers, a hosted evening wine reception, yoga accessories upon request, and Aveeda bath products. The Grace Slick suite offers a unique slice of rock 'n' roll history. The excellent Grand Café is adjacent and provides 24-hour room service. Wheelchair-accessible.

Petite Auberge $$$–$$$$$ *863 Bush Street, SF 94102, tel: 415-928-6000, tel: 800-365-3004 (toll-free in US), www.jdvhospitality.com.* A very romantic B&B, with a full breakfast served in a homey dining room as well as complimentary afternoon tea and cookies and evening hors d'oeuvres and wine. The less expensive rooms have showers only; the high-end rooms are large with full baths, and all are very comfortable. Book ahead.

Hotel Rex $$$–$$$$$ *562 Sutter Street, SF 94102, tel: 415-433-4434, tel: 800-433-4434 (toll-free in US), www.jdvhospitality.com.* With a nod to the 1930s, the sophisticated Rex is dedicated to the literati and hosts book signings, poetry readings and jazz on Fridays at the Library Bar, where classic American cuisine is served. An evening wine hour, morning coffee, newspapers, and Wi-fi are all complimentary.

The Ritz-Carlton, San Francisco $$$$–$$$$$ *600 Stockton Street, SF 94108, tel: 415-296-7465, tel: 800-241-3333 (toll-free in US), www.ritzcarlton.com.* Once the giant neoclassical corporate headquarters of an insurance company, it is now a luxury hotel catering to those with deep pocketbooks. Opened in 1991, the Ritz offers enormous rooms, a fitness center, indoor pool, fine dining restaurant, and primo service. Wheelchair-accessible.

Sir Francis Drake $$$–$$$$$ *450 Powell Street, SF 94102, tel: 415-392-7755, tel: 800-795-7129 (toll-free in US), www.sirfrancis drake.com.* Glide past the uniformed valets into the grand lobby of this 1928 landmark building. A $20 million renovation refurbished all guestrooms and public spaces. The excellent Scala's Bistro is located next door, and there's a popular nightclub with a spectacular view on the top floor. Wheelchair-accessible.

Hotel Triton $$$–$$$$ *342 Grant Avenue, SF 94108, tel: 415-394-0500, tel: 800-800-1299 (toll-free in US), www.hoteltriton.com.* Rock music greets patrons entering this trendy hotel just across the street from the Chinatown Dragon Gate. The wild designs and mod furniture scattered around the lobby are amusing, but guestrooms are small. The Triton is eco-friendly: they have a sophisticated recycling program, use biodegradable cleaning products, energy-efficient systems, recycled paper, and other environmentally conscious practices.

Warwick Regis $$–$$$ *490 Geary Street, SF 94102, tel: 415-928-7900, tel: 800-203-3232 (toll-free in US), www.warwickhotels.com.* Guests receive all the amenities expected of a much larger hotel, like marble-tiled baths, afternoon tea and cookies, same-day laundry service, and 24-hour room service. All the elegantly appointed guestrooms are quiet. The Union Square location is especially convenient for theater-goers.

Westin St Francis $$$$ *335 Powell Street, SF 94102, tel: 415-397-7000, tel: 866-500-0338 (toll-free in US), www.westinstfrancis.com.* The location, across the street from Union Square, adds to the excitement of staying at this legendary hotel: if the historic aspects interest you, reserve a room in the original building, they're furnished with handsome reproductions and chandeliers. Amenities include an on-site fitness center, room service, and the urbane Clock Bar completes the package. Wheelchair-accessible.

NOB HILL

Huntington Hotel $$$$$ *1075 California Street, SF 94108, tel: 415-474-5400, tel: 800-227-4683 (toll-free in US), www.huntington hotel.com.* A refined family-owned hotel built in 1924 at the top of Nob Hill, it is discreetly luxurious if a little faded. Originally an apartment building, the rooms are larger than average. For great views, be sure to ask for a room above the eighth floor. The Nob Hill Spa on the premises is one of the city's best.

Inter-Continental Mark Hopkins $$$$$ *1 Nob Hill, SF 94108, tel: 415-392-3434, tel: 800-662-4455 (toll-free in US), www.san-francisco.intercontinental.com.* At the summit of Nob Hill, with grand views in all directions, this hotel offers luxury rooms on the site of the original Mark Hopkins mansion. The rooftop cocktail lounge, Top of the Mark, has been a city tradition since 1939, and an atmosphere of quiet refinement prevails throughout. Sip one of their famous martinis while you enjoy the top-class jazz. Wheelchair-accessible.

Hotel Vertigo $–$$$ *940 Sutter Street, SF, 94109, tel: 888-444-4605, www.hotelvertigosf.com.* Located on the site of the Empire Hotel made famous by Alfred Hitchcock's film *Vertigo*, which was partially shot in San Francisco, this affordable hotel has a whimsical attitude and style that borders on kitschy. Some rooms have flat screen TVs and refrigerators. The lower Nob Hill location is a bit sketchy, but also convenient.

White Swan Inn $$$–$$$$$ *845 Bush Street, SF 94108, tel: 415-775-1755, tel: 800-999-9570 (toll-free in US), www.jdvhospitality.com.* A cozy English-style bed and breakfast inn. The romantic rooms and suites all have fireplaces stave off the infamous San Francisco chill. A gourmet breakfast buffet is served daily. Afternoon tea with home-baked cookies and evening wine and hors d'oeuvres are served in the parlor. A two-night minimum stay is usually required.

THE EMBARCADERO

Harbor Court Hotel $$–$$$$ *165 Steuart Street, SF 94105, tel: 415-882-1300, tel: 866-792-6283 (toll-free in US), www.harborcourthotel.com.* Across from the Rincon Center, this 1907 building with bay views has been converted into an elegant boutique hotel with small but comfortable rooms and varied luxury amenities. Guests have complimentary access to the state-of-the-art fitness center next door. Wheelchair-accessible.

Hyatt Regency San Francisco $$$–$$$$$ *5 Embarcadero Center, SF 94111, tel: 415-788-1234, tel: 800-233-1234 (toll-free in US), www.sanfranciscoregency.hyatt.com.* The location at the foot of Market Street is good for walkers and public transportation. Some great restaurants are close by. Big rooms, fitness center, the works. Wheelchair-accessible.

SOMA

InterContinental San Francisco $$–$$$ *888 Howard Street, SF 94103, tel: 415-616-6500, www.intercontinentalsanfrancisco.com.* Sleek, sexy, and technologically sophisticated, this 32-story highrise is befitting of secret agents and supermodels. A sumptuous spa offers every service imaginable and the hotel bar boasts a collection of 200 grappas. Luce, a Michelin-starred restaurant rounds out the experience.

Hotel Milano $$$–$$$$ *55 Fifth Street, SF 94103, tel: 415-543-8555, tel: 800-398-7555 (toll-free in US), www.hotelmilanosf.com.* The location – next door to the San Francisco Centre, a few blocks from Yerba Buena Gardens and the Moscone Center, and close to several museums including SFMOMA – makes this hotel a good pick for the motivated sightseer. An on-site fitness room, restaurant, and full service make up for the spare decor. Wheelchair-accessible.

Hotel Palomar $$$ *12 Fourth Street, SF 94103, tel: 415-348-1111, www.hotelpalomar-sf.com.* The comfortable rooms here have bold, colorful accents in an artsy hotel that is chock full of amenities like an evening wine reception, morning coffee, tea, and newspapers, and bicycles loaned for day use. The acclaimed Fifth Floor restaurant is located within.

MARINA

Hotel Del Sol $$ *3100 Webster Street, SF 94123, tel: 415-921-5520, tel: 877-433-5765 (toll-free in US), www.jdvhospitality.com.* Once a boring Lombard Street motel, the Del Sol had a radical makeover and proves that looks are almost everything. Color is used to great effect, splashed on walls, fabrics, and mosaic tiles that decorate tabletops and walkways. Comfortable medium- to large-sized rooms surround a heated swimming pool, small lawn and hammock; suites are available, and parking is free. Wheelchair-accessible.

The Marina Inn $–$$ *3110 Octavia, SF 94123, tel: 415-928-1000, tel: 800-274-1420 (toll-free in US), www.marinainn.com.* This is an inexpensive, gracious Victorian inn off Lombard Street, not far from the Golden Gate Bridge, the Presidio, and the upscale shopping on Union and Chestnut streets. The rooms are simply furnished with an old-fashioned feel; the inside rooms are considerably quieter, but don't have much natural light. A continental breakfast is included in the price. Wheelchair-accessible.

NORTH BEACH/FISHERMAN'S WHARF

Hotel Bohème $$–$$$ *444 Columbus Street, SF 94133, tel: 415-433-9111, www.hotelboheme.com.* A flight of narrow stairs brings you inside this delightful small hotel in the heart of North Beach. Iron beds and brightly painted walls grace the small but lovely bedrooms, and the baths are well stocked with toiletries. The front-desk staff is happy to assist with rental cars, dinner reservations, and tours. All rooms have free Wi-fi.

San Remo Hotel $ *2337 Mason Street, SF 94133, tel: 415-776-8688, tel: 800-352-7366 (toll-free in US), www.sanremohotel.com.* Built right after the 1906 earthquake, it originally served as a boarding house for sailors, poets, and pensioners, and was a speakeasy during Prohibition. Today it's a bargain, with a stellar location and immaculate rooms. Some share bathroom facilities. The penthouse is a treat, and Fior d'Italia, the restaurant on the first floor, is the stuff of North Beach legend.

Tuscan Inn $$$–$$$$$ *425 North Point, SF 94133, tel: 415-561-1100, tel: 800-648-4626 (toll-free in US), www.tuscaninn.com.* Of the many hotels around Fisherman's Wharf, this is a solid choice. The concierge is enthusiastic and helpful, the attractive rooms are well sized by local standards, and the location is appealing to families who wish to be near Pier 39. Wheelchair-accessible.

WESTERN ADDITION (ALAMO SQUARE)

The Metro Hotel 319 $ *Divisadero Street, SF 94117, tel: 415-861-5364, www.metrohotelsf.com.* A ridiculously affordable hotel in the central and increasingly trendy NoPa (north of the Panhandle) location, just steps from Haight Street. Don't look for amenities here. Rooms are small and sometimes noisy, but clean. The private garden is inviting. Lots of groovy bars and inexpensive food options, including a great vegan restaurant, are nearby.

HAIGHT-ASHBURY

The Red Victorian Bed & Breakfast Inn $–$$ *1665 Haight Street, SF 94117, tel: 415-864-1978, www.redvic.com.* The Summer of Love is alive and well at this peace haven on Haight Street. Reasonably priced '60s-themed rooms some with private baths, canopied beds, colorful quilts and tie-dyed fabrics. No televisions, but plenty of good vibes.

The Stanyan Park Hotel $$–$$$$$ *750 Stanyan Street, SF 94117, tel: 415-751-1000, www.stanyanpark.com.* An elegant and affordable early 20th-century boutique hotel located across the street from Golden Gate Park. Suites (with full kitchens, living and dining rooms, and pull-out sofas) are large and ideal for families and long-term stays. Free Wi-Fi. Continental breakfast included.

INDEX

Berlitz pocket guide

San Francisco

Tenth Edition 2012

Written by Paula Tevis
Updated by Lisa Dion
Series Editor: Tom Stainer

Photography
All photography by Richard and Daniella Nowitz/APA except AKG 17, 21; Chris Coe 22; 37, 77; Everynight images 88; Tony Halliday/APA 53; iStockphoto 24; Fotolia 1; Randy Wilder/Monterey Bay Aquarium 81; Thomas Gilcrease Institute of American History & Art, Tulsa, Oklahoma 19;

Cover picture: 4Corners Images

Contact us

At Berlitz we strive to keep our guides as accurate and up to date as possible, but if you find anything that has changed, or if you have any suggestions on ways to improve this guide, then we would be delighted to hear from you.

Berlitz Publishing, PO Box 7910, London SE1 1WE, England.
email: berlitz@apaguide.co.uk
www.berlitzpublishing.com

Printed in China by CTPS

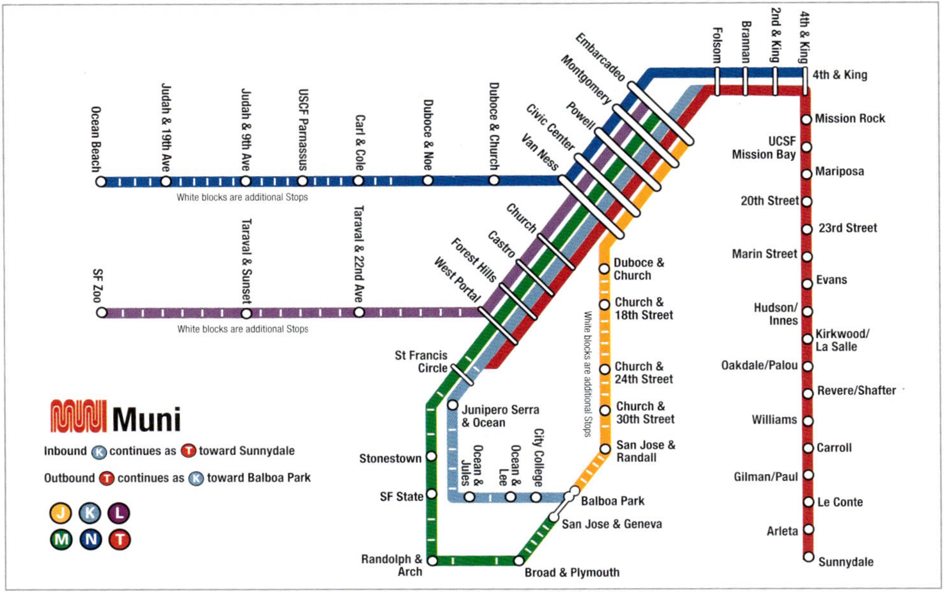
Muni
Inbound K continues as T toward Sunnydale
Outbound T continues as K toward Balboa Park
J K L
M N T
4th & King
2nd & King
Brannan
Folsom
Embarcadeo
Montgomery
Powell
Civic Center
Van Ness
Church
Castro
Forest Hills
West Portal
St Francis Circle
Mission Rock
UCSF Mission Bay
Mariposa
20th Street
23rd Street
Marin Street
Evans
Hudson/ Innes
Kirkwood/ La Salle
Oakdale/Palou
Revere/Shafter
Williams
Carroll
Gilman/Paul
Le Conte
Arleta
Sunnydale
Duboce & Church
Church & 18th Street
Church & 24th Street
Church & 30th Street
San Jose & Randall
White blocks are additional Stops
Balboa Park
San Jose & Geneva
Broad & Plymouth
City College
Ocean & Lee
Ocean & Jules
Junipero Serra & Ocean
Stonestown
SF State
Randolph & Arch
Duboce & Church
Duboce & Noe
Carl & Cole
USCF Parnassus
Judah & 9th Ave
Judah & 19th Ave
Ocean Beach
White blocks are additional Stops
Taraval & 22nd Ave
Taraval & Sunset
SF Zoo
White blocks are additional Stops